The Essential Motivation Handbook

The Essential Motivation Handbook

Leo Babauta and Eric Hamm

WAKING LION PRESS

ISBN 978-1-4341-0319-2

Published by Waking Lion Press, an imprint of The Editorium

The Editorium, LLC
West Valley City, UT 84128-3917
wakinglionpress.com
wakinglion@editorium.com

Contents

Introduction

By Leo Babauta

I've long wanted to put together a motivation ebook—I get emails and comments from readers every day in need of motivation to reach a goal, to stay focused, to exercise, to be productive, to just get up off their butts and do something.

But I wanted to add something, add value greater than I already offer on Zen Habits.

And so I turned to Eric Hamm of the Motivate Thyself blog, and found the perfect partner for this book.

Eric writes about motivation all the time—it's the lifeblood of his blog, and what he lives every day. He knows motivation as well as I do.

The two of us have accomplished a lot, working for others and working for ourselves. We've had plenty of failures, and through these failures have learned tons about motivation, and about ourselves.

It's from these failures that we've gathered the attitudes and methods that actually work, that have given us the motivation needed to achieve our goals.

It's our hope that we'll pass on some of this practical advice to you, and that you'll go on to use it to achieve great things yourself. Even if you've already achieved great things, at the very least I know this ebook will serve as a basic reminder and give you a little shove when you need it.

I recommend using this ebook like this: read it in little bits, and put them into action. And when you need a bit of motivation, pull it up and read some more, and then get your butt into action again.

Good luck, my friends, and may all your dreams become reality!

—Leo

Chapter 1

How To Motivate Yourself

By Eric Hamm

How to motivate yourself?" is a question that only *you* know the answer to. Hidden deep inside all of us is both the desire to do great things and the knowledge to strive for them. But for many of us, these are things that are buried beyond our normal understanding of ourselves. So if you want to know how to motivate yourself, you have to first learn a bit more *about* yourself.

FIRST: WHAT IS MOTIVATION?

Think about a car, sitting on a flat, paved road. The engine's not running and the break is not engaged. Your job is to push the car past a certain point. So you lean into it and start pushing with all your might. At first it's barely budging, but then starts creeping ahead. You dig deep and give it all you've got. The tires start to make their way around and the car starts moving forward. Now your energy is beginning to transfer from brute force to a kind of flow. The further you push the car, the easier it gets as momentum starts to make its way into the scenario. The motivation was the act of breaking the barrier between frozen and forward motion. Once that took place, momentum was born and your energy enhanced. So if you want to know how to motivate yourself, you'll need to decipher your own personal tricks for breaking that barrier.

SECOND: KNOW WHAT TRULY TURNS YOU ON!

When I was a car salesman, my manager always tried to motivate us with money. I remember one specific instance when I had been working really hard and was looking forward to the following day as it was my day off. There was a big sale going on and the more salesman on the lot, the better it was for the dealership. So my manager came up to me with a kind of evil grin and said, "You gonna be here tomorrow?" (He knew it was my day off.) "Because you'll sure make a killing if you *are* here!" In my mind I just rolled my eyes as I *hate* being manipulated, but the point is, my manager just didn't know my hot spots. Sure, I like money and all that, but I cherish my time much more. If he had honestly come up to me and said something like, "Hey Eric, I know you're off tomorrow, but we could really use you on the lot. And if it helps, you'll probably make some good money, which never hurts. But I totally understand if you can't make it." I may not have come in either way, but that kind of honest request lights a fire inside me that is much more likely to drive me to action, than just shaking some cash in front of my face. So if you want to know how to motivate yourself, you've got to know your *real* hot buttons. I have been the one to dangle money in front of my face many times, only to crash and burn when my drive shows its shallowness. But when I hit on what *truly* matters to me, nothing can slow me down.

THIRD: FOCUS ON MAKING THE CAR MOVE, NOT ON MOVING THE CAR.

Going back to the 'car pushing' scenario, I want to point out the importance of short sided thinking when it comes to motivating yourself. Focus takes energy and energy is the resource that starts the car moving. If our focus is spread out, our energy will be weak. So we can't afford to worry about anything *after* the car starts to move. That part will take care of itself. (ADHD moment . . .) It's kind of like a magnifying glass in the sun. If the glass was flat and therefore spreads the light equally over the object in its path, nothing would happen. But by manipulating the glass to focus the light onto a pinpointed area, you harness all the power that the light has to offer, creating a powerful beam. So if you want to know how to motivate yourself, you have to stop concerning yourself with the whole process. Your job is to *just* break that 'freeze barrier.'

FOURTH: YOU'VE GOT TO CUT THE FAT!

Do you ever have those times in your life when even a few common tasks feel like a strain? Chances are, you're bearing the weight of so many invisible burdens that *everything* is a challenge. How can you put *all* your energy into starting that motion if half of it is being drained by these unnecessary burdens? I'm not suggesting that we can go throughout life, totally care free and lightly loaded, but much of what we willingly take on becomes a burden, not a future asset. Look at your days, see what takes up your time and determine the value of these tasks. Then cut those responsibilities that drain more than they produce. (Another ADHD moment . . .) You know when you get a new computer and there's all that CRAPware preloaded on it? You know, those free trials of this and advertisements of that? And you know how sluggish everything runs because of it? Then you uninstall all the junk and suddenly your computer feels fast and efficient, the way you expected it to. Well this is precisely how many of us live. Loaded down with good intentions and what seemed like good ideas, we sluggishly go through our days, wondering why we can't get anything done. So if you want to know how to motivate yourself, you need to go to 'Add/Remove Programs' and take care of some business. Unless, of course, you have a Mac. Then you can just sit there and laugh at the Windows users. :-D

FIFTH: LEARN TO USE PAST MOTION FOR FUTURE MOTIVATION.

I like to run during the winter. It's easy to do when it's cold outside and a great way to get some fresh air. But if I get out of this healthy habit, I find it much harder to act on. But if I can push through a few sessions, I find that the ones ahead are much more fluid. One positive makes the possibility of a second much more viable. Five, even more so. So if you want to know how to motivate yourself, you need to learn the magic of momentum as you harness the power of your past positive motion.

Chapter 2

The Only Two Secrets to Motivating Yourself You'll Ever Need

By Leo Babauta

I've written about motivation a bunch of times before, but the more I learn about it, the more I realize that motivation isn't that complicated.

Sure, there are numerous tips that can help, numerous tactics and strategies I've used with success. But it really all boils down to two things.

And those two things are so deceptively simple that you might decide to stop reading after I name them: 1) make things enjoyable and 2) use positive public pressure. But read on for more on how to use those two things to motivate yourself for any goal.

IT'S MOTIVATION, NOT DISCIPLINE

First let's back up a little bit. A number of readers have emailed me about sticking to their goals—anything from exercise and eating right to being organized and productive to creating new habits—and have said they simply lack the discipline to stick with things for very long.

But what is discipline, really? It's mostly an illusion, in my experience. When people say that someone has "discipline," as I've written about before, they really mean he has the motivation to stick to something.

Let's take the example of someone in the military, a typical case of somone who is said to have discipline. This military man might get up super early, fix his bed neatly, go on an early-morning run, do a bunch of other exercises, and generally do a disciplined job throughout the day.

But is that just because he's disciplined? I think it's mostly because he's in a situation where there's public pressure (both positive and negative) to do all of the things listed above. If he doesn't do them, he might get yelled at or demerited or look bad in front of his peers. If he does do them, he's an exemplary soldier.

There's also the fact that after awhile, these things become pleasurable for him. He gets a sense of satisfaction out of staying in shape and keeping things neat. He enjoys the early morning. He feels good about being conscientious about his job.

So in the end, it's not some vague quality ("discipline") that allows him to stick to these habits, but rather the two secrets of motivation: positive public pressure and enjoyment.

WHAT I LEARNED FROM MY EXPERIENCES

Over the last few years, I've been experimenting with achieving various goals—from waking early to exercising to eliminating my debt and living frugally and simply and more. And what I've learned has repeatedly taught me that these two key motivation principles are all you need.

I've learned other things as well, but the more I stick to my goals, the more I realize that it's these two themes that keep repeatedly surfacing. It's almost eerie, actually. Just a few goals as illustration:

• Marathon. Right now I'm training for my third marathon, in Honolulu this December. As I've stuck with the toughest marathon plan I've ever undertaken (last week my longer runs were 12 and 20 miles, and this week I'm doing 2 runs of 14 miles), I've marveled at my ability to keep at it. But it's not hard to figure out why: I've publicly committed to doing this marathon—on this blog, on Twitter and on Train For Humanity, where I'm raising money for humanitarian causes through my training. In addition to that, I'm really enjoying all the running!

• Blogging. I've now been blogging for almost two years (I started in January 2007), making Zen Habits one of the longest-running projects I've ever stuck with. I've worked on many projects before, but they are usually completed within a year, if not within a few weeks or months. Anything longer is usually intimidating to me. But it hasn't taken discipline to stick with blogging, not at all. It's something I really enjoy, and there's the added bonus of positive public pressure that has motivated me to stick with it.

• Writing a book. A couple months ago, I finished the manuscript for my book, The Power of Less, that's coming out at the end of this year. I will admit that I had some trouble writing this book, with the demands of publishing a blog (two blogs actually), training for my second marathon in March, and preparing for my wedding in June. I wasn't always following my own advice (although in my defense I learned to segregate the different goals so I only concentrated on one at a time). But I did get the book done with both forms of motivation—pressure from my publisher to turn in the manuscript, and the enjoyment I got from writing the book once I was able to clear away distractions and focus on the writing. I could go into many more examples of how I used these two forms of motivation, but you get the idea. Now let's take a look at each one and how you can use them to your advantage.

POSITIVE PUBLIC PRESSURE

While pressure is often seen as a bad thing ("I'm under too much pressure!"), if used properly it can actually be a good thing. It's important that pressure not be applied in too negative a way and too high an intensity. Keep things positive and at a manageable intensity, and things will move along nicely.

Some examples of how to use positive public pressure to motivate yourself:

• Tell all your co-workers you're going to achieve a goal ("No sugary snacks this week!" or "I'm going to keep my email inbox completely empty") and report to them regularly on your progress.

• Email your family and friends and tell them about your goal and ask them to keep you accountable. Email them regular updates, and tell them about your progress when you see them.

• Post your goal on your blog and post regular updates. It's important that you not just post the goal but also stay accountable with the updates. Encourage people to ask you about your goal if you don't report your progress.

• Join an online forum related to your goal—I've done this when I quit smoking and also when I started running. Introduce yourself, make friends, tell them about your goal, ask for help when you need it, and report your successes and failures.

• Write a regular column in a publication on your goal. I did this when I ran my first marathon, for my local newspaper. It created a lot of positive public pressure—everywhere I went, people would say, "Hey, you're that marathon guy! How's the running going?" Of course, not everyone can write a column for a newspaper, but you could do it for a group blog or a newsletter or some other type of publication.

• Post your goal and a chart of your progress up in your office or other public place.

• Post pictures of yourself each day. One guy did this and created a video of his progress—it was amazing to watch. You get the idea. I'm sure you can come up with some ideas of your own.

Enjoy Your Goal Activity

You can motivate yourself to do something you don't like to do, using positive public pressure as motivation. But if you really don't enjoy it, you'll only be able to keep it up for so long. And even if you could do it for months and years . . . is that something you'd want to do? If you don't enjoy it, why do it for very long?

But, you might say, what if it's something I really want to achieve but I don't enjoy it? There are ways to find enjoyment in most things—the key is to focus on the enjoyable parts. Focus on the positive.

Here are some ways to use this motivational principle to your advantage:

• Having trouble motivating yourself to write for your blog? Look for topics that excite you. If you find things that you're passionate about, writing becomes easy.

• Having trouble with a dissertation for graduate school? Maybe you're not as passionate about the topic as you thought you were. Re-examine your dissertation topic and see if you can either re-energize yourself about it or find a new topic you can get excited about.

• Having a hard time exercising? Find exercise that's fun for you. If you don't like running, try soccer or basketball or rowing. If you don't like to lift weights, try doing some primal workouts where you flip logs and jump through tires. Go hiking. Walk with friends and talk the whole time.

• Is eating healthy a challenge for you? Find healthy foods you love. Experiment with new recipes and have fun testing them out.

• Is training for a marathon tough? Learn to enjoy the quiet of the early morning, the contemplative nature of running, or the beautiful nature that surrounds you. Or play some songs that pump you up. Or listen to interesting audiobooks as you run.

Find the enjoyable parts of any activity, and focus on those. In time, you can really learn to love something. Or, switch to something you love more and stick to that.

These two principles, especially when used together, can be powerful motivators. In fact, in most cases, they're all the motivation I ever need.

Chapter 3

A Guide to Beating the Fears That Are Holding You Back

By Leo Babauta

"Every time we choose safety, we reinforce fear." —*Cheri Huber*

Fear of something bad happening in the future is one of the things that make us human. Animals might fear an immediate danger, that is happening right now, but only we fear something that might happen, that isn't happening now, that isn't even showing its ugly face at the moment.

This fear, some might say, is necessary . . . it stops us from doing something stupid. But I've found most of these fears to be unnecessary, to be baseless, to be holding us back from achieving something.

I recently asked my Twitter friends: "What fear is holding you back?" Their responses included:
- failure
- abandonment/rejection
- intimacy
- success
- being broke
- not being good enough I think the last one—not being good enough—is actually at the root of all the others. We fear we'll fail because we're not good enough. We fear we'll lose our relationships, that we'll be abandoned, that we'll

be rejected . . . because we're not good enough. We fear intimacy for the very same reason—we might get rejected because we're not good enough. Even the fear of success is based on the worry that we're not good enough. Do you have this fear? That you're not good enough? I have, for all my life, and I still have it today.

But here's the thing: having the fear is natural. Letting it stop you from going after your dreams is a tragedy.

I did this, for well over a decade of my adult life. I let the fear of not being good enough stop me from even trying, from even daring to dream.

It turned out that my fears were baseless. I am good enough. I'm not perfect, but who is? When I was able to overcome this fear of not being good enough, this fear of failure and rejection, and put myself out there in the world, I succeeded. I found out that I was good enough.

And I still have this same fear—I still worry that I'm not good enough, that I'll fail and flop on my face in front of 100,000 people . . . but I wouldn't be human if I didn't. Even the most successful people—Barack Obama, Steve Jobs, Paul McCartney, J.K. Rowling, et al—they have this fear, even if they don't show it. But they don't let it hold them back.

How can you do this? Let's look into it.

"The greatest barrier to success is the fear of failure." —Sven Goran Eriksson

How to Beat Your Fears

There is no step-by-step program to beating your fears, but here's what I've learned, first-hand and from others.

1. First, acknowledge your fear. This is a huge first step. If you do just this today, you've done something great. Many of us have these fears, but they are at the back of our mind, unnoticed, unacknowledged, as we try to ignore them and

pretend they're not there. But they are there. And they affect us, every day, all our lives. So acknowledge the fear.

2. Write it down. What's your fear? Write it on a piece of paper. Writing it down not only acknowledges that you have it—bringing it out into the light—but it externalizes the fear. It takes the fear from the dark lurking places in the back of your mind, where it has power over you, out into the light of day, outside of you, where you have power over the fear. Take control over it by writing it down. It is now outside you. You can do something about it. I personally like to crumple it up and stomp on it, but you can do whatever you like. Post it on your fridge as a reminder of your enemy.

3. Feel the fear. You've acknowledged it, but you're still afraid of it. You're reluctant to even have this fear, perhaps even embarrassed about it. Well, no more. Recognize that you're not alone, that we *all* have these fears, that we all think we might not be good enough. Yes, even the amazing Barack Obama, the amazing Jessica Alba, the amazing Al Pacino. They have the same fears as you do. I sure do. Repeat after me: there's nothing wrong with having this fear. Now allow yourself to feel it. Experience it fully. Bask in this fear. It isn't as bad as you think. It's a part of you, but it doesn't control you. From djbarker on Twitter: "Feel the fear & do it anyway."

4. Ask yourself: what's the worst thing that can happen? Often it's not as bad as we think. Do you fear failing in a new career? What would happen if you did? You'd get another job. You'd move on. You'd live. Do you fear being rejected by someone of the opposite sex? What would happen if you were? You'd lick your wounds, you'd find someone else who is more suited for you, you'd live. Do you fear being broke? What would happen if you were? You'd cut back on your expenses, perhaps ask family or friends to help you out for a little bit. You'd find a way to make money. You'd live.

5. Just do it. To repeat: feel the fear and do it anyway. To beat the fear, you have to just do it. See below for some tips on doing this, but what works for me is not thinking, just acting. Like when you want to jump off a waterfalls into the pool below: don't think about it. Just jump! It's an exhilarating feeling. I fear public speaking, but when I get up and just do it, I feel great. From Jade Craven on Twitter: "I fear everything. I've recently decided to ignore my fears and just go for it! So many opportunities have come as a result."

6. Prepare yourself for battle. When you're going to take on an adversary, you prepare yourself. You arm yourself, and have a battle plan, and train yourself. Do this in your battle against your fear: arm yourself, have a battle plan, train yourself. If you want to be a musician but you fear failure . . . practice, practice, practice, then come up with a plan to succeed, then get all the skills and info you need to implement the plan, then practice some more. Then go out and implement the plan!

7. Be in the moment. Fear of failure (and other similar fears) are fears of the future. We get caught up in worrying about what might happen. Instead, banish all thoughts of the future. Banish even thoughts of past mistakes and failures. Now focus on right now. Do something right now to beat your fears, to pursue your dreams, and forget about what might happen. Just do it, now, in the moment. When you find yourself thinking about the past or future, bring yourself back in the moment and focus on what you're doing right at this moment.

8. Small steps. Conquering fear and pursuing a life goal can be overwhelming, intimidating. So start small. Just take one little baby step. Something you know you can do. Something you're sure to succeed at. Then feel good about that (see below) and take another small baby step. Keep doing this, and soon you'll have conquered a mountain.

9. Celebrate every success! Every single thing you do right, celebrate! Even the smallest little thing. And use this feeling of success, of victory, to propel yourself forward and take the next step. Bill Gates describes a "spiral of success" that he used to build Microsoft up from its early success of MS-DOS, to its success with Windows and Word and Excel and Internet Explorer and all that (I know, blech, but still). Use this idea of a spiral of success in your life—build upon each success, use it as a stepping stone to the next victory.

"To conquer fear is the beginning of wisdom." —Bertrand Russell

Chapter 4

Task Ninja: Form the Action Habit

By Leo Babauta

A lot of us get stuck in inaction–procrastinating, doing a lot of unimportant tasks to avoid the important stuff, worrying about failing or about being perfect, having a hard time starting, getting distracted, and so on.

It's time to start forming the Action Habit instead.

And it's really not that hard if you focus on it for a little while. Like any other habit, start in small doses, little tasks, just short bursts, and then build on that momentum.

SOME QUICK STEPS FOR FORMING THE ACTION HABIT

1. Figure out your key actions. Focusing on the right actions is just as important as the doing. Don't spend a lot of time in this step—just quickly decide your Top 3 actions for today.

2. Pick one key action, and visualize the outcome. How will it look when you're done? Again, don't spend a lot of time here—just form a quick picture in your mind.

3. Just start. Tell yourself, "Do it now!" Make it a mantra. Don't mess around with tools, with distractions, with anything that will get in the way of doing this task. Strip away everything but the task, and get going!

4. Focus on the moment. Just be in this task, don't worry about the future or what mistakes you might make or might

have made before. Just focus on doing this task, as best you can. Immerse yourself in it.

5. Get to done. Complete the task. Feel good about it! Pat yourself on the back! Now repeat with the next task. The more you practice this habit, the better you get. Do it in small doses, and keep practicing. You'll fail sometimes. See the next section for how to deal with that. But don't let failure stop you—just practice some more.

BARRIERS TO THE ACTION HABIT

But what if you're having trouble actually taking action? Some quick thoughts:

• Don't worry about perfect. Too often we want to create the perfect plan, but while it's important to know where you're going, it's more important not to get stuck in the planning mode. And while it's important to do your best, perfection isn't necessary.

• Stop fiddling. Are you messing around with your software or other tools? Are you playing with fonts and colors and other non-essential things? Stop! Get back to the task.

• Remove distractions. Turn off the phone, email, IM, Twitter, etc. Shut off the world around you, and just focus on the doing.

• Improve it later. Just do it now. You can make it better later. Writers call this the sh•tty first draft—and while it sounds bad, it's actually a good thing. You're getting it done, even if it's sloppy.

• Break it into smaller chunks. Sometimes the task is too intimidating. If the task takes more than an hour, start with a 30-minute chunk. If that's too big, do just 10 minutes. If that's too hard, do 5. If you have to, just do 1 minute, just to get going.

• Stop thinking so much. Thinking is a good thing. Over-thinking isn't, and it gets in the way. Put aside all the thinking (analysis paralysis) and just do.

- If you can't do something . . . figure out why. Maybe you don't have the tools. Maybe you don't have the authority. Maybe you need something from someone else. Maybe you're missing some key info. Maybe you don't know how to do something and need to read up on it, or be taught how. Maybe you just don't want to do it, and you should drop it altogether. Figure out what the barrier is, and solve it.

Chapter 5

Top 20 Motivation Hacks

By Leo Babauta

Achieving goals is not a matter of having "discipline." It's a matter of motivating yourself, and keeping your focus on your goal. Follow these hacks, or any combination of them that works for you, and you should have the motivation and focus you need.

Here they are, in reverse order:

20. Chart your progress. Recently I posted about how I created a chart to track my progress with each of my goals. This chart is not just for information purposes, for me to look back and see how I'm doing. It's to motivate me to keep up with my goals. If I'm diligent about checking my chart every day, and marking dots or "x"s, then I will want to make sure I fill it with dots. I will think to myself, "I'd better do this today if I want to mark a dot." Well, that's a small motivation, but it helps, trust me. Some people prefer to use gold stars. Others have a training log, which works just as well. Or try Joe's Goals. However you do it, track your progress, and allow yourself a bit of pride each time you give yourself a good mark.

Now, you will have some bad marks on your chart. That's OK. Don't let a few bad marks stop you from continuing. Strive instead to get the good marks next time.

19. Hold yourself back. When I start with a new exercise

program, or any new goal really, I am rarin' to go. I am full of excitement, and my enthusiasm knows no boundaries. Nor does my sense of self-limitation. I think I can do anything. It's not long before I learn that I do have limitations, and my enthusiasm begins to wane. Well, a great motivator that I've learned is that when you have so much energy at the beginning of a program, and want to go all out—*hold back*. Don't let yourself do everything you want to do. Only let yourself do 50–75 percent of what you want to do. And plan out a course of action where you slowly increase over time. For example, if I want to go running, I might think I can run 3 miles at first. But instead of letting myself do that, I start by only running a mile. When I'm doing that mile, I'll be telling myself that I can do more! But I don't let myself. After that workout, I'll be looking forward to the next workout, when I'll let myself do 1.5 miles. I keep that energy reined in, harness it, so that I can ride it even further.

18. Join an online (or off-line) group to help keep you focused and motivated. When I started to run, more than a year ago, I joined a few different forums, at different times, on different sites, such as Men's Health (the Belly-Off Runner's Club), Runner's World, Cool Running, and the running group at About.com. I did the same when I was quitting smoking.

Each time I joined a forum, it helped keep me on track. Not only did I meet a bunch of other people who were either going through what I was going through or who had already been through it, I would report my progress (and failures) as I went along. They were there for great advice, for moral support, to help keep me going when I wanted to stop.

17. Post a picture of your goal someplace visible—near your desk or on your refrigerator, for example. Visualizing your goal, exactly how you think it will be when you've achieved it, whether it's financial goals like traveling to Rome or building a dream house, or physical goals like finishing a

marathon or getting a flat stomach, is a great motivator and one of the best ways of actualizing your goals.

Find a magazine photo or a picture online and post it somewhere where you can see it not only daily, but hourly if possible. Put it as your desktop photo, or your home page. Use the power of your visual sense to keep you focused on your goal. Because that focus is what will keep you motivated over the long term—once you lose focus, you lose motivation, so having something to keep bringing your focus back to your goal will help keep that motivation.

16. Get a workout partner or goal buddy. Staying motivated on your own is tough. But if you find someone with similar goals (running, dieting, finances, etc.), see if they'd like to partner with you. Or partner with your spouse, sibling or best friend on whatever goals they're trying to achieve. You don't have to be going after the same goals—as long as you are both pushing and encouraging each other to succeed.

15. Just get started. There are some days when you don't feel like heading out the door for a run, or figuring out your budget, or whatever it is you're supposed to do that day for your goal. Well, instead of thinking about how hard it is, and how long it will take, tell yourself that you just have to start.

I have a rule (not an original one) that I just have to put on my running shoes and close the door behind me. After that, it all flows naturally. It's when you're sitting in your house, thinking about running and feeling tired, that it seems hard. Once you start, it is never as hard as you thought it would be. This tip works for me every time.

14. Make it a pleasure. One reason we might put off something that will help us achieve our goal, such as exercise for example, is because it seems like hard work. Well, this might be true, but the key is to find a way to make it fun or pleasurable. If your goal activity becomes a treat, you actually look forward to it. And that's a good thing.

13. Give it time, be patient. I know, this is easier said than done. But the problem with many of us is that we expect quick results. When you think about your goals, think long term. If you want to lose weight, you may see some quick initial losses, but it will take a long time to lose the rest. If you want to run a marathon, you won't be able to do it overnight. If you don't see the results you want soon, don't give up . . . give it time. In the meantime, be happy with your progress so far, and with your ability to stick with your goals. The results will come if you give it time.

12. Break it into smaller, mini goals. Sometimes large or longer-term goals can be overwhelming. After a couple weeks, we may lose motivation, because we still have several months or a year or more left to accomplish the goal. It's hard to maintain motivation for a single goal for such a long time. Solution: have smaller goals along the way.

11. Reward yourself. Often. And not just for longer-term goals, either. I've talked about breaking larger goals into smaller, mini goals. Well, each of those mini goals should have a reward attached to it. Make a list of your goals, with mini goals, and next to each, write down an appropriate reward. By appropriate, I mean 1) it's proportionate to the size of the goal (don't reward going on a 1-mile run with a luxury cruise in the Bahamas); and 2) it doesn't ruin your goal—if you are trying to lose weight, don't reward a day of healthy eating with a dessert binge. It's self-defeating.

10. Find inspiration, on a daily basis. Inspiration is one of the best motivators, and it can be found everywhere. Every day, seek inspiration, and it will help sustain motivation over the long term. Sources of inspiration can include: blogs, on-line success stories, forums, friends and family, magazines, books, quotes, music, photos, people you meet.

9. Get a coach or take a class. These will motivate you to at least show up, and to take action. It can be applied to any

goal. This might be one of the more expensive ways of motivating yourself, but it works. And if you do some research, you might find some cheap classes in your area, or you might know a friend who will provide coaching or counseling for free.

8. Have powerful reasons. Write them down. Know your reasons. Give them some thought . . . and write them down. If you have loved ones, and you are doing it for them, that is more powerful than just doing it for self-interest. Doing it for yourself is good too, but you should do it for something that you *really really* want to happen, for really good reasons.

7. Become aware of your urges to quit, and be prepared for them. We all have urges to stop, but they are mostly unconscious. One of the most powerful things you can do is to start being more conscious of those urges. A good exercise is to go through the day with a little piece of paper and put a tally mark for each time you get an urge. It simply makes you aware of the urges. Then have a plan for when those urges hit, and plan for it beforehand, and write down your plan, because once those urges hit, you will not feel like coming up with a plan.

6. Make it a rule never to skip two days in a row. This rule takes into account our natural tendency to miss days now and then. We are not perfect. So, you missed one day . . . now the second day is upon you and you are feeling lazy . . . tell yourself *No!* You will not miss two days in a row! Zen Habits says so! And just get started. You'll thank yourself later.

5. Visualize your goal clearly, on a daily basis, for at least 5–10 minutes. Visualize your successful outcome in great detail. Close your eyes, and think about exactly how your successful outcome will look, will feel, will smell and taste and sound like. Where are you when you become successful? How do you look? What are you wearing? Form as clear a mental picture as possible. Now here's the next key: do it every day.

For at least a few minutes each day. This is the only way to keep that motivation going over a long period of time.

4. Keep a daily journal of your goal. If you are consistent about keeping a journal, it can be a great motivator. A journal should have not only what you did for the day, but your thoughts about how it went, how you felt, what mistakes you made, what you could do to improve. To be consistent about keeping a journal, do it right after you do your goal task each day. Make keeping a journal a sensory pleasure.

3. Create a friendly, mutually-supportive competition. We are all competitive in nature, at least a little. Some more than others. Take advantage of this part of our human nature by using it to fuel your goals. If you have a workout partner or goal buddy, you've got all you need for a friendly competition. See who can log more miles, or save more dollars, each week or month. See who can do more pushups or pullups. See who can lose the most weight or have the best abs or lose the most inches on their waist. Make sure the goals are weighted so that the competition is fairly equal. And mutually support each other in your goals.

2. Make a big public commitment. Be fully committed. This will do the trick every time. Create a blog and announce to the world that you are going to achieve a certain goal by a certain date. Commit yourself to the hilt.

1. Always think positive. Squash all negative thoughts. Monitor your thoughts. Be aware of your self-talk. We all talk to ourselves, a lot, but we are not always aware of these thoughts. Start listening. If you hear negative thoughts, stop them, push them out, and replace them with positive thoughts. Positive thinking can be amazingly powerful.

Chapter 6

The Ultimate Guide to Motivation—How to Achieve Any Goal

By Leo Babauta

"Obstacles are those frightful things you see when you take your eyes off your goal." —Henry Ford

One of the biggest challenges in meeting any goal, whether it be related to productivity, waking early, changing a habit, exercising, or just becoming happier, is finding the motivation to stick with it.

If you can stick with a goal for long enough, you'll almost always get there eventually. It just takes patience, and motivation.

Motivation is the key, but it's not always easy, day in and day out, to find that motivation.

What follows is a guide to motivation using what I've learned over the last few years in a series of successful accomplishments, goals and habit changes. I've had many failures, but also many successes, and I've learned a lot from all of them. Motivation has been a particularly important topic of exploration for me.

WHAT MOTIVATION CAN ACHIEVE

What have I accomplished using these motivation methods? Too much to mention, just in the last 3 years: running two marathons, learning to become an early riser, losing 40 pounds, completing a triathlon, becoming vegetarian, becoming more productive, starting a successful blog, writing a book, becoming organized, simplifying my life, quitting my day job, tripling my income, eliminating my debt, and much more.

That's not intended to sound like bragging, but to show you what can be accomplished (just to start) if you find the right motivation.

HOW DOES MOTIVATION WORK?

Before we get into specific methods, it's useful to examine what motivation is, what it does, and how it works.

Motivation is what drives you toward a goal, what keeps you going when things get tough, the reason you get up early to exercise or work late to finish a project. There are all kinds of motivations, of course, from positive to negative. Having a boss threaten to fire you is motivation—you'll likely work harder to complete a project with that kind of pressure. But I find that positive motivation works better—if it's something you really want to do, you'll do a much better job than to avoid something you don't want (such as being fired).

So motivation, in its best form, is a way for you to want to do something. There may be times, for example, when you don't feel like getting up early, and in those times you may seriously just want to sleep in (not that there's anything wrong with that). But if you have a reason to want to get up early, something you really really want to do, you'll jump up out of bed with excitement.

The best motivation, then, is a way for you to really want something, to get excited about it, to be passionate about it.

Remember that, as there are many other types of motivation (especially negative), but in my experience, this is the kind that works the best.

There is only so long that you can go trying to motivate yourself to do something you don't like to do, something you don't want to do. But if you find ways to really want to do something, you can sustain your effort for much, much longer.

8 Ways to Motivate Yourself From the Beginning

I've found that it's important to start out with the right motivation, because a good start can build momentum that you can sustain for a long time. If you start out right, you have a much better chance of succeeding. Here are some tips for starting out:

1. Start small. I've said this before, but that's because it's one of the most important tips in motivating yourself toward a goal. Don't start out big! Start out with a ridiculously easy goal, and then grow from there. If you want to exercise, for example, you may be thinking that you have to do these intense workouts 5 days a week. No—instead, do small, tiny, baby steps. Just do 2 minutes of exercise. I know, that sounds wimpy. But it works. Commit to 2 minutes of exercise for one week. You may want to do more, but just stick to 2 minutes. It's so easy, you can't fail. Do it at the same time, every day. Just some crunches, 2 pushups, and some jogging in place. Once you've done 2 minutes a day for a week, increase it to 5, and stick with that for a week. In a month, you'll be doing 15–20. Want to wake up early? Don't think about waking at 5 A.M. Instead, think about waking 10 minutes earlier for a week. That's all. Once you've done that, wake 10 minutes earlier than that. Baby steps.

2. One goal. Too many people start with too many goals at once, and try to do too much. And it saps energy and moti-

vation. It's probably the most common mistake that people make. You cannot maintain energy and focus (the two most important things in accomplishing a goal) if you are trying to do two or more goals at once. It's not possible—I've tried it many times. You have to choose one goal, for now, and focus on it completely. I know, that's hard. Still, I speak from experience. You can always do your other goals when you've accomplished your One Goal.

3. Examine your motivation. Know your reasons. Give them some thought . . . and write them down. If you have loved ones, and you are doing it for them, that is more powerful than just doing it for self-interest. Doing it for yourself is good too, but you should do it for something that you *really really* want to happen, for really good reasons.

4. Really, really want it. This is essentially the same as the above tip, but I want to emphasize it: it's not enough to think it would be cool to achieve something. It has to be something you're passionate about, something you're super excited about, something you want deeply. Make sure that your goal meets these criteria, or you won't stick with it for long.

5. Commit publicly. None of us likes to look bad in front of others. We will go the extra mile to do something we've said publicly. For example, when I wanted to run my first marathon, I started writing a column about it in my local daily newspaper. The entire island of Guam (pop. 160K) knew about my goal. I couldn't back down, and even though my motivation came and went, I stuck with it and completed it. Now, you don't have to commit to your goal in your daily newspaper, but you can do it with friends and family and co-workers, and you can do it on your blog if you have one. And hold yourself accountable—don't just commit once, but commit to giving progress updates to everyone every week or so.

6. Get excited. Well, it starts with inspiration from others (see above), but you have to take that excitement and build

on it. For me, I've learned that by talking to my wife about it, and to others, and reading as much about it as possible, and visualizing what it would be like to be successful (seeing the benefits of the goal in my head), I get excited about a goal. Once I've done that, it's just a matter of carrying that energy forward and keeping it going.

7. Build anticipation. This will sound hard, and many people will skip this tip. But it really works. It helped me quit smoking after many failed attempts. If you find inspiration and want to do a goal, don't start right away. Many of us will get excited and want to start today. That's a mistake. Set a date in the future—a week or two, or even a month—and make that your Start Date. Mark it on the calendar. Get excited about that date. Make it the most important date in your life. In the meantime, start writing out a plan. And do some of the steps below. Because by delaying your start, you are building anticipation, and increasing your focus and energy for your goal.

8. Print it out, post it up. Print out your goal in big words. Make your goal just a few words long, like a mantra ("Exercise 15 mins. Daily"), and post it up on your wall or refrigerator. Post it at home and work. Put it on your computer desktop. You want to have big reminders about your goal, to keep your focus and keep your excitement going. A picture of your goal (like a model with sexy abs, for example) also helps.

20 WAYS TO SUSTAIN MOTIVATION WHEN YOU'RE STRUGGLING

The second half of motivation is to keep yourself going when you don't feel the same excitement as you did in the beginning. Perhaps something new has come into your life and your old goal isn't as much of a priority anymore. Perhaps you skipped a day or two and now you can't get back into it. Perhaps you screwed up and got discouraged.

If you can get yourself excited again, and keep going, you'll get there eventually. But if you give up, you won't. It's your choice—accomplish the goal, or quit. Here's how you can stop from quitting, and get to your goal:

1. Hold yourself back. When I start with a new exercise program, or any new goal really, I am rarin' to go. I am full of excitement, and my enthusiasm knows no boundaries. Nor does my sense of self-limitation. I think I can do anything. It's not long before I learn that I do have limitations, and my enthusiasm begins to wane. Well, a great motivator that I've learned is that when you have so much energy at the beginning of a program, and want to go all out—*hold back*. Don't let yourself do everything you want to do. Only let yourself do 50–75 percent of what you want to do. And plan out a course of action where you slowly increase over time. For example, if I want to go running, I might think I can run 3 miles at first. But instead of letting myself do that, I start by only running a mile. When I'm doing that mile, I'll be telling myself that I can do more! But I don't let myself. After that workout, I'll be looking forward to the next workout, when I'll let myself do 1.5 miles. I keep that energy reined in, harness it, so that I can ride it even further.

2. Just start. There are some days when you don't feel like heading out the door for a run, or figuring out your budget, or whatever it is you're supposed to do that day for your goal. Well, instead of thinking about how hard it is, and how long it will take, tell yourself that you just have to start. I have a rule that I just have to put on my running shoes and close the door behind me. After that, it all flows naturally. It's when you're sitting in your house, thinking about running and feeling tired, that it seems hard. Once you start, it is never as hard as you thought it would be. This tip works for me every time.

3. Stay accountable. If you committed yourself publicly, through an online forum, on a blog, in email, or in person . . .

stay accountable to that group of people. Commit to report back to them daily, or something like that, and stick to it! That accountability will help you to want to do well, because you don't want to report that you've failed.

4. Squash negative thoughts and replace them with positive ones. This is one of the most important motivation skills, and I suggest you practice it daily. It's important to start monitoring your thoughts, and to recognize negative self-talk. Just spend a few days becoming aware of every negative thought. Then, after a few days, try squashing those negative thoughts like a bug, and then replacing them with a corresponding positive thought. Squash, "This is too hard!" and replace it with, "I can do this! If that wimp Leo can do it, so can I!" It sounds corny, but it works. Really.

5. Think about the benefits. Thinking about how hard something is is a big problem for most people. Waking early sounds so hard! Just thinking about it makes you tired. But instead of thinking about how hard something is, think about what you will get out of it. For example, instead of thinking about how hard it is to wake early, focus on how good you'll feel when you're done, and how your day will be so much better. The benefits of something will help energize you.

6. Get excited again! Think about why you lost your excitement . . . then think about why you were excited in the first place. Can you get that back? What made you want to do the goal? What made you passionate about it? Try to build that up again, refocus yourself, get energized.

7. Read about it. When I lose motivation, I just read a book or blog about my goal. It inspires me and reinvigorates me. For some reason, reading helps motivate and focus you on whatever you're reading about. So read about your goal every day, if you can, especially when you're not feeling motivated.

8. Find like-minded friends. Staying motivated on your own is tough. But if you find someone with similar goals

(running, dieting, finances, etc.), see if they'd like to partner with you. Or partner with your spouse, sibling or best friend on whatever goals they're trying to achieve. You don't have to be going after the same goals—as long as you are both pushing and encouraging each other to succeed. Other good options are groups in your area (I'm part of a running club, for example) or online forums where you can find people to talk to about your goals.

9. Read inspiring stories. Inspiration, for me, comes from others who have achieved what I want to achieve, or who are currently doing it. I read other blogs, books, magazines. I Google my goal, and read success stories. Zen Habits is just one place for inspiration, not only from me but from many readers who have achieved amazing things. I love, love, love reading success stories too.

10. Build on your successes. Every little step along the way is a success—celebrate the fact that you even started! And then did it for two days! Celebrate every little milestone. Then take that successful feeling and build on it, with another baby step. Add 2–3 minutes to your exercise routine, for example. With each step (and each step should last about a week), you will feel even more successful. Make each step really, really small, and you won't fail. After a couple of months, your tiny steps will add up to a lot of progress and a lot of success.

11. Just get through the low points. Motivation is not a constant thing that is always there for you. It comes and goes, and comes and goes again, like the tide. But realize that while it may go away, it doesn't do so permanently. It will come back. Just stick it out and wait for that motivation to come back. In the meantime, read about your goal, ask for help, and do some of the other things listed here until your motivation comes back.

12. Get help. It's hard to accomplish something alone. When I decided to run my marathon, I had the help of friends

and family, and I had a great running community on Guam who encouraged me at 5K races and did long runs with me. When I decided to quit smoking, I joined an online forum and that helped tremendously. And of course, my wife Eva helped every step of the way. I couldn't have done these goals without her, or without the others who supported me. Find your support network, either in the real world or online, or both.

13. Chart your progress. This can be as simple as marking an X on your calendar, or creating a simple spreadsheet, or logging your goal using online software. But it can be vastly rewarding to look back on your progress and to see how far you've come, and it can help you to keep going—you don't want to have too many days without an X! Now, you will have some bad marks on your chart. That's OK. Don't let a few bad marks stop you from continuing. Strive instead to get the good marks next time.

14. Reward yourself often. For every little step along the way, celebrate your success, and give yourself a reward. It helps to write down appropriate rewards for each step, so that you can look forward to those rewards. By appropriate, I mean 1) it's proportionate to the size of the goal (don't reward going on a 1-mile run with a luxury cruise in the Bahamas); and 2) it doesn't ruin your goal—if you are trying to lose weight, don't reward a day of healthy eating with a dessert binge. It's self-defeating.

15. Go for mini-goals. Sometimes large or longer-term goals can be overwhelming. After a couple weeks, we may lose motivation, because we still have several months or a year or more left to accomplish the goal. It's hard to maintain motivation for a single goal for such a long time. Solution: have smaller goals along the way.

16. Get a coach or take a class. These will motivate you to at least show up, and to take action. It can be applied to any goal. This might be one of the more expensive ways

of motivating yourself, but it works. And if you do some research, you might find some cheap classes in your area, or you might know a friend who will provide coaching or counseling for free.

17. Never skip two days in a row. This rule takes into account our natural tendency to miss days now and then. We are not perfect. So, you missed one day . . . now the second day is upon you and you are feeling lazy . . . tell yourself *No!* You will not miss two days in a row!

18. Use visualization. Visualize your successful outcome in great detail. Close your eyes, and think about exactly how your successful outcome will look, will feel, will smell and taste and sound like. Where are you when you become successful? How do you look? What are you wearing? Form as clear a mental picture as possible. Now here's the next key: do it every day. For at least a few minutes each day. This is the only way to keep that motivation going over a long period of time.

19. Be aware of your urges to quit, and overcome them. We all have urges to stop, but they are mostly unconscious. One of the most powerful things you can do is to start being more conscious of those urges. A good exercise is to go through the day with a little piece of paper and put a tally mark for each time you get an urge. It simply makes you aware of the urges. Then have a plan for when those urges hit, and plan for it beforehand, and write down your plan, because once those urges hit, you will not feel like coming up with a plan.

20. Find pleasure again. No one can stick to something for long if they find it unpleasant, and are only rewarded after months of toil. There has to be fun, pleasure, joy in it, every day, or you won't want to do it. Find those pleasurable things—the beauty of a morning run, for example, or the satisfaction in reporting to people that you finished another step along the way, or the deliciousness of a healthy meal.

"Never, never, never, never give up." —Winston Churchill

Chapter 7

Progress, Progress, Progress! 5 Tips To Keep You Moving Forward

By Eric Hamm

I was reminded of a valuable fact, recently, when it comes to staying motivated so you can keep moving forward. I had a lot of projects on my plate right and I was putting in a lot of "overtime." Though some days I was a little tired, I was making a lot of progress and felt great. One day, things were no different, except for one big difference. I got a " great idea" for one of the websites I've been working on. It had to do with a lot of complicated, time consuming work that may or may not have been such a "great idea" anyway. It involved purchasing some software and, after I had some issues activating it, I ended up spending a couple of hours on web forums trying to resolve the issue.

About halfway through this whole ordeal I got this gut feeling that I was really sliding backwards. After weeks of really making some progress and feeling great because of it, I realized that I had let myself become distracted. And that this distraction was starting to undo the progress I had made. In the past I may have continued with the mess and tried to "resolve" it but I instead decided to go with my gut, backtrack to the point that I had started to go off course, and continue with my journey in a positive direction.

I returned the software and just looked at the wasted time

as a lesson learned and hopefully one that will keep me from making the same mistake in the future. The big realization that I came to was the fact that forward progress brings on a sense of hope in reaching your goals which feeds your motivation and aids your success in life. But getting sidetracked by something that is not helping you reach your goals is a sure fire way of becoming discouraged and losing site of what you had set out to do. Because once you stop making progress, you will most definitely start to backslide into the mediocrity that you see all around you. This journey isn't about moving forward or standing still. It's more like being on a treadmill. It takes some effort to just keep from falling back, let alone making progress.

So here are 5 tips that I came away with in my struggle for forward progress.

1. Wear blinders if you have to. My mistake was not keeping my eyes on the prize. I had a set goal when I was in the store but I let myself go off track to "play with some ideas." This was when I went off course. Try not to let yourself become distracted by all that is around you. You will always be bombarded with advertising of every kind. There will always be something you "have to have" or that will most certainly "enhance your life." But most of the time these are just things that will pull you away from what's really important. So be very diligent in keeping your eyes on the prize.

2. Be aware of the time. This is just a simple, yet very important, tip. All too often, even when working on something important, we lose track of time and get less accomplished because of it. Be careful not to let yourself become too engrossed in any one task or you will run the risk of neglecting another. Progress is made by getting things done. If you get lost in what you do you will most certainly get less done overall.

3. Do it and be done with it. In light of tip #2, this one will help you get the job done. When working toward a goal

it is important not to be too picky. Let's say you are work-ing on a new logo for a website. Yes, it's important that it looks good but you shouldn't spend all day working on it. Anything can be tweaked "just a little bit more." I have a tendency to be the one who keeps on tweaking. But all that "finalizing" can really take away from the progress you could have made on other tasks. Just realize this fact; most things need a rough and final draft. The rough draft gets the task done while the final draft cleans it up. These two steps are necessary to accomplishing the task. Beyond that you are just treading water.

4. Listen to your gut. If I hadn't done this I would have been continuing down the road to progress derailment. The first thing you need to do though, is be aware of what the right situation feels like so you will know the wrong one when it comes. How can you know if it's dark out if you don't know what light looks like? Next time you are in a great place in life and making great strides in progress, take note of your gut feeling. This will be your neutral spot. Any-thing more positive than this is great. But anything less is potentially a backslide. I'm not saying you can't have your bad days. Just be aware of your situation so that you can maintain your forward heading.

5. Don't be afraid to backtrack. This final tip is greatly im-portant. All too often we find ourselves stuck in that place where the only way to move forward is to first move back-ward. Just like hiking on a trail, if you were to get lost, you might find that you need to backtrack so you can return to making forward progress. Often times though, we will just keep moving off course, hoping to eventually run back into the path. This rarely works and usually ends up getting you more off course. So don't be afraid to turn around and go back way you came. It may at first feel counter productive, but you will be glad you did it once you get back on course.

And while you are working your way back you can use the time to reflect on the importance of maintaining a positive heading.

I hope these tips are helpful to you as you seek your goals and pursue your dreams. Feel free to add to them with your comments and let me know how *you* stay on track.

Chapter 8

7 Steps to Turn Your Self-Improvement Desires Into Reality

By Leo Babauta

"Reality leaves a lot to the imagination." —John Lennon

How many times have we told ourselves in complete earnestness, "I'm going to be more organized and productive from now on."? Or that the diet starts tomorrow? Or that we're going to make a real effort to exercise now?

Only to have that enthusiasm fizzle away, and all our best intentions come to nothing? It's the most common thing in the world (besides bacteria)—the honest and fervent desire for self-improvement, followed by inaction or giving in to temptations, followed by guilt or giving up. Bridget Jones captured it best, writing her constant resolutions into her diary. "Will definitely go to the gym this afternoon." Only to be followed by a binge of pastries followed by drinking and smoking.

We're all Bridget Jones. It happens to the best of us. It's inertia at work, mixed with a bit of laziness as well as the very human trait of giving in to desires despite all the good intentions in the world.

So how do we beat inertia and temptations? Four basic ways, really:

1. Get moving, a bit at a time. Inertia is beat only by move-

ment. Once you get going, momentum builds up and inertia is no longer a factor. So the key is to get started, and you do that not by trying to go from 0 to 60 in 5 seconds, but by trying to go from 0 to 5mph in a day or two. That's doable. It's all about baby steps. Once you get going, you're golden.

2. Be accountable. Laziness, the second culprit, is beat by a bit of public pressure. We all get lazy from time to time (or, to be more honest, all the time), and there's nothing wrong with that. But to beat laziness, we must apply a bit of pressure, in the form of accountability. There's nothing wrong with a little pressure, as long is it's not overdone. Pressure is a motivating thing, especially when it's positive. Positive pressure includes encouragement from family or friends, an online forum, a help group in your neighborhood, or the readers of your blog.

3. Ignore failures—giving in to temptation is OK. We will always give in to temptation. Plan for it, accept it, move on. There's no need to beat yourself up.

4. Motivate yourself. Most importantly, you want to really want it. It's not enough to feel pressure to do something— you have to really desire it. I mean, really desire it, not just think it's something you should do, or that you'll be a better person for doing it. If pressure gives you the push toward your goal, motivation gives you the pull.

Given those strategies for beating the obstacles to making your desires become reality . . . how do we implement them? How do we go from theory to actual action steps? Easy. Seven simple steps, that you can do today. Really. Do them today.

1. Make a date. Right now. All the good intentions in the history of the universe mean nothing if you don't actually get started. And the only way to get started is to take action, right now. Not tomorrow, not later today, not in an hour, not when you finish reading this article. Right now! Look at your calendar, and make an appointment to create your action

plan, or to take the first action ("Go walking at 5:30 P.M. today in the park," for example). What's the first action you can take to make your desires a reality? Create a healthier meal plan for tomorrow? Create a place for everything you use at work, so your organizing system doesn't fall apart in two day? Decide what that is and make an appointment for it, right now. Second part of this step: make that appointment the most important appointment on your schedule, more important than a doctor's appointment or a meeting with your boss.

2. Set a small, achievable goal. Remember, inertia is a powerful force. If you haven't been exercising for a couple years, it's hard to get started. You're used to the way things are, and even if you want to change, it's difficult. So don't start out trying to conquer the world. Just conquer something exceedingly small. It might sound wimpy to say, "I'm going to walk for 10 minutes" or "I'm going to do 10 pushups and 1 chinup," but those are much more likely to beat inertia than, "I'm going to exercise for 45 minutes today." Be realistic, and make it very very achievable. It's the only way to beat inertia.

"Try not. Do or do not. There is no try." —Yoda in The Empire Strikes Back.

3. Commit thyself, big time. It's this commitment that will keep you going after you overcome inertia. Sometimes we get filled up with enthusiasm, but then a few days later, that enthusiasm wanes and we submit to our old buddy laziness. Now, I'm not anti-laziness—just the opposite, I assure you— but we can't let it stop us from making our dreams come true. So instead, make a commitment, publicly. State your small, achievable goal, and tell it to as many people as you can. Call or email friends and family, tell all your coworkers, join an online forum related to your goal and tell all of them. Put it on your blog. However you do it, make sure people

are aware of your goal, and that there's sufficient pressure to overcome laziness.

4. Baby steps, baby. Again, inertia is a very strong force. I've said it before, but this is a very important step here: the best way to change is through baby steps. One small step at a time. Don't try to bite off too much. How is this different from the above step, setting a small and achievable goal? It's the same concept, but extended beyond the initial goal. It's taking things one little goal at a time, a bit at a time. For example, let's say you want to run a marathon, but currently your running regimen consists of running to the bathroom during commercial breaks while you're watching Lost. So do you go out and start a marathon training plan? Nope. You start by walking 10 minutes a day. Then, when that becomes a habit and too easy, walk 15 minutes. Then 20, then 30. Then jog a minute, walk a couple minutes, jog a minute, and so on, for those 30 minutes. Then jog 90 seconds, and so on, until you're running for 30 minutes. Do these steps a week or two at a time, so that all of a sudden, you're running for 45 minutes every other day . . . and you barely noticed the progression.

That's the way you get to a goal . . . small progressions that are barely noticeable. Not by killing yourself the first day out.

"Seventy percent of success in life is showing up." —Woody Allen

5. Hold thyself accountable. You've committed yourself publicly . . . but it's not enough to tell people your goal. You have to make it clear that they must hold you accountable to reporting to them your progress. Then report your progress to them regularly. Daily is better than weekly. Reporting to them makes sure that you will think twice about being lazy and forgoing your action plan.

6. Motivate yourself. We've already discussed accountability and commitment, which are ways to put positive pressure

on yourself—a form of motivation. Those are great, but you also want other types of motivation. You want to find ways to make your progress feel great . . . either through rewards, or the positive way you feel about your progress, or the positive way you feel when others see how well you're doing. Find a few different ways to motivate yourself—the more the better. Incorporate these into your plan. Tell people about them. Let them help push you along.

7. Just keep doing it, no matter what. You'll encounter obstacles, and falter and fall. Just get up and keep going. You'll face temptations and give in. That's OK. Just keep going. You'll make mistakes and get discouraged. No matter . . . just keep going. Learn from your mistakes, and . . . keep going. No matter what happens, keep going. If you're taking baby steps, you're holding yourself accountable, and you're actually doing something, you'll get there.

"Reality is merely an illusion, albeit a very persistent one"
—Albert Einstein

Chapter 9

25 Killer Actions to Boost Your Self-Confidence

By Leo Babauta

"Once we believe in ourselves, we can risk curiosity, wonder, spontaneous delight, or any experience that reveals the human spirit." —E.E. Cummings

One of the things that held me back from pursuing my dreams for many years was fear of failure . . . and the lack of self- confidence that I needed to overcome that fear.

It's something we all face, to some degree, I think. The key question: how do you overcome that fear? By working on your self-confidence and self-esteem. Without really thinking of it in those terms, that's what I've been doing over the years, and that's what helped me finally overcome my fears, and finally pursue my dreams.

I still have those fears, undoubtedly. But now I know that I can beat them, that I can break through that wall of fear and come out on the other side. I've done it many times now, and that success will fuel further success.

This chapter was inspired by reader Nick from Finland, who asked for an article about self-worth and self-confidence:

Many of the things you propose make people feel better about themselves and actually help building self-confidence.

However, I would be interested on reading your input in general on this topic. Taking time out for your own plans and dreams, doing things another way than most other people and generally not necessarily "fitting in" can be quite hard with a low self-confidence.

Truer words have never been spoken. It's near impossible to make time for your dreams, to break free from the traditional mold, and to truly be yourself, if you have low self-esteem and self-confidence.

As an aside, I know that some people make a strong distinction between self-esteem and self-confidence. In this article, I use them interchangeably, even if there is a subtle but perhaps important difference . . . the difference being whether you believe you're worthy of respect from others (self-esteem) and whether you believe in yourself (self-confidence). In the end, both amount to the same thing, and in the end, the actions I mention below give a boost to both self-esteem and self- confidence.

TAKING CONTROL OF YOUR SELF-CONFIDENCE

If you are low in self-confidence, is it possible to do things that will change that? Is your self-confidence in your control?

While it may not seem so, if you are low in self-confidence, I strongly believe that you can do things to increase your self- confidence. It is not genetic, and you do not have to be reliant on others to increase your self-confidence. And if you believe that you are not very competent, not very smart, not very attractive, etc. . . . that can be changed.

You can become someone worthy of respect, and someone who can pursue what he wants despite the naysaying of others.

You can do this by taking control of your life, and taking control of your self-confidence. By taking concrete actions that improve your competence, your self-image, you can increase that self-confidence, without the help of anyone else.

Below, I outline 25 things that will help you do that. None of them is revolutionary, none of them will do it all by themselves. The list certainly isn't comprehensive. These are just some of my favorite things, stuff that's worked for me.

And you don't need to do all of them, as if this were a recipe . . . pick and choose those that appeal to you, maybe just a couple at first, and give them a try. If they work, try others. If they don't, try others. Here they are, in no particular order:

1. Groom yourself. This seems like such an obvious one, but it's amazing how much of a difference a shower and a shave can make in your feelings of self-confidence and for your self-image. There have been days when I turned my mood around completely with this one little thing.

2. Dress nicely. A corollary of the first item above . . . if you dress nicely, you'll feel good about yourself. You'll feel successful and presentable and ready to tackle the world. Now, dressing nicely means something different for everyone . . . it doesn't necessarily mean wearing a $500 outfit, but could mean casual clothes that are nice looking and presentable.

3. Photoshop your self-image. Our self-image means so much to us, more than we often realize. We have a mental picture of ourselves, and it determines how confident we are in ourselves. But this picture isn't fixed and immutable. You can change it. Use your mental Photoshopping skills, and work on your self-image. If it's not a very good one, change it. Figure out why you see yourself that way, and find a way to fix it.

4. Think positive. One of the things I learned when I started running, about two years ago, what how to replace negative thoughts (see next item) with positive ones. How I can actually change my thoughts, and by doing so make

great things happened. With this tiny little skill, I was able to train for and run a marathon within a year. It sounds so trite, so Norman Vincent Peale, but my goodness this works. Seriously. Try it if you haven't.

5. Kill negative thoughts. Goes hand-in-hand with the above item, but it's so important that I made it a separate item. You have to learn to be aware of your self-talk, the thoughts you have about yourself and what you're doing. When I was running, sometimes my mind would start to say, "This is too hard. I want to stop and go watch TV." Well, I soon learned to recognize this negative self-talk, and soon I learned a trick that changed everything in my life: I would imagine that a negative thought was a bug, and I would vigilantly be on the lookout for these bugs. When I caught one, I would stomp on it (mentally of course) and squash it. Kill it dead. Then replace it with a positive one. ("C'mon, I can do this! Only one mile left!")

"Know yourself and you will win all battles." —Sun Tzu

6. Get to know yourself. When going into battle, the wisest general learns to know his enemy very, very well. You can't defeat the enemy without knowing him. And when you're trying to overcome a negative self-image and replace it with self-confidence, your enemy is yourself. Get to know yourself well. Start listening to your thoughts. Start writing a journal about yourself, and about the thoughts you have about yourself, and analyzing why you have such negative thoughts. And then think about the good things about yourself, the things you can do well, the things you like. Start thinking about your limitations, and whether they're real limitations or just ones you've allowed to be placed there, artificially. Dig deep within yourself, and you'll come out (eventually) with even greater self-confidence.

7. Act positive. More than just thinking positive, you have to put it into action. Action, actually, is the key to develop-

ing self-confidence. It's one thing to learn to think positive, but when you start acting on it, you change yourself, one action at a time. You are what you do, and so if you change what you do, you change what you are. Act in a positive way, take action instead of telling yourself you can't, be positive. Talk to people in a positive way, put energy into your actions. You'll soon start to notice a difference.

8. Be kind and generous. Oh, so corny. If this is too corny for you, move on. But for the rest of you, know that being kind to others, and generous with yourself and your time and what you have, is a tremendous way to improve your self-image. You act in accordance with the Golden Rule, and you start to feel good about yourself, and to think that you are a good person. It does wonders for your self-confidence, believe me.

"One important key to success is self-confidence. A key to self-confidence is preparation." —Arthur Ashe

9. Get prepared. It's hard to be confident in yourself if you don't think you'll do well at something. Beat that feeling by preparing yourself as much as possible. Think about taking an exam: if you haven't studied, you won't have much confidence in your abilities to do well on the exam. But if you studied your butt off, you're prepared, and you'll be much more confident. Now think of life as your exam, and prepare yourself.

10. Know your principles and live them. What are the principles upon which your life is built? If you don't know, you will have trouble, because your life will feel directionless. For myself, I try to live the Golden Rule and fail often). This is my key principle, and I try to live my life in accordance with it. I have others, but they are mostly in some way related to this rule (the major exception being to "Live my Passion"). Think about your principles . . . you might have them but perhaps you haven't given them much thought. Now think

about whether you actually live these principles, or if you just believe in them but don't act on them.

11. Speak slowly. Such a simple thing, but it can have a big difference in how others perceive you. A person in authority, with authority, speaks slowly. It shows confidence. A person who feels that he isn't worth listening to will speak quickly, because he doesn't want to keep others waiting on something not worthy of listening to. Even if you don't feel the confidence of someone who speaks slowly, try doing it a few times. It will make you feel more confident. Of course, don't take it to an extreme, but just don't sound rushed either.

12. Stand tall. I have horrible posture, so it will sound hypocritical for me to give this advice, but I know it works because I try it often. When I remind myself to stand tall and straight, I feel better about myself. I imagine that a rope is pulling the top of my head toward the sky, and the rest of my body straightens accordingly. As an aside, people who stand tall and confident are more attractive. That's a good thing any day, in my book.

13. Increase competence. How do you feel more competent? By becoming more competent. And how do you do that? By studying and practicing. Just do small bits at a time. If you want to be a more competent writer, for example, don't try to tackle the entire profession of writing all at once. Just begin to write more. Journal, blog, write short stories, do some freelance writing. The more you write, the better you'll be. Set aside 30 minutes a day to write (for example), and the practice will increase your competence.

14. Set a small goal and achieve it. People often make the mistake of shooting for the moon, and then when they fail, they get discouraged. Instead, shoot for something much more achievable. Set a goal you know you can achieve, and then achieve it. You'll feel good about that. Now set another small goal and achieve that. The more you achieve small

goals, the better you'll be at it, and the better you'll feel. Soon you'll be setting bigger (but still achievable) goals and achieving those too.

15. Change a small habit. Not a big one, like quitting smoking. Just a small one, like writing things down. Or waking up 10 minutes earlier. Or drinking a glass of water when you wake up. Something small that you know you can do. Do it for a month. When you've accomplished it, you'll feel like a million bucks.

16. Focus on solutions. If you are a complainer, or focus on problems, change your focus now. Focusing on solutions instead of problems is one of the best things you can do for your confidence and your career. "I'm fat and lazy!" So how can you solve that? "But I can't motivate myself!" So how can you solve that? "But I have no energy!" So what's the solution?

17. Smile. Another trite one. But it works. I feel instantly better when I smile, and it helps me to be kinder to others as well. A little tiny thing that can have a chain reaction. Not a bad investment of your time and energy.

18. Volunteer. Related to the "be kind and generous" item above, but more specific. It's the holiday season right now . . . can you find the time to volunteer for a good cause, to spread some holiday cheer, to make the lives of others better? It'll be some of the best time you've ever spent, and an amazing side benefit is that you'll feel better about yourself, instantly.

19. Be grateful. I'm a firm believer in gratitude, as anyone who's been reading this blog for very long knows well. But I put it here because while being grateful for what you have in life, for what others have given you, is a very humbling activity . . . it can also be a very positive and rewarding activity that will improve your self-image.

20. Exercise. Gosh, I seem to put this one on almost every list. But if I left it off this list I would be doing you a

disservice. Exercise has been one of my most empowering activities in the last couple years, and it has made me feel so much better about myself. All you have to do is take a walk a few times a week, and you'll see benefits.

21. Empower yourself with knowledge. Empowering yourself, in general, is one of the best strategies for building self-confidence. You can do that in many ways, but one of the surest ways to empower yourself is through knowledge. This is along the same vein as building competence and getting prepared . . . by becoming more knowledgeable, you'll be more confident . . . and you become more knowledgeable by doing research and studying. The Internet is a great tool, of course, but so are the people around you, people who have done what you want, books, magazines, and educational institutions.

22. Do something you've been procrastinating on. What's on your to-do list that's been sitting there? Do it first thing in the morning, and get it out of the way. You'll feel great about yourself.

23. Get active. Doing something is almost always better than not doing anything. Of course, doing something could lead to mistakes . . . but mistakes are a part of life. It's how we learn. Without mistakes, we'd never get better. So don't worry about those. Just do something. Get off your butt and get active—physically, or active by taking steps to accomplish something.

24. Work on small things. Trying to take on a huge project or task can be overwhelming and daunting and intimidating for anyone, even the best of us. Instead, learn to break off small chunks and work in bursts. Small little achievements make you feel good, and they add up to big achievements. Learn to work like this all the time, and soon you'll be a self-confident maniac.

25. Clear your desk. This might seem like a small, simple thing (then again, for some of you it might not be so small).

But it has always worked wonders for me. If my desk starts to get messy, and the world around me is in chaos, clearing off my desk is my way of getting a little piece of my life under control. It is the calm in the center of the storm around me.

"Somehow I can't believe that there are any heights that can't be scaled by a man who knows the secrets of making dreams come true. This special secret, it seems to me, can be summarized in four C s. They are curiosity, confidence, courage, and constancy, and the greatest of all is confidence. When you believe in a thing, believe in it all the way, implicitly and unquestionably." —Walt Disney

Chapter 10

6 Small Things You Can Do When You Lack Discipline

By Leo Babauta

One of the biggest problems people face is the lack of discipline—they have goals or habits they want to achieve, but lack that discipline needed to stick with it.

Then we beat ourselves up about it. We feel crappy because we can't stick with it. And that leads to more failure, because we're forming a mindset that we don't have the necessary discipline. Here's what to do when you face a situation like this:

1. Forgive yourself. You aren't perfect. No one is. Realize that beating yourself up will only make things worse. Take a few slow, deep breaths and let it go. Forgive yourself. And move on.

2. Realize that discipline is an illusion. While discipline is a common concept, it doesn't actually exist. It's not a thing you can actually do. Think about it: people say discipline is pushing yourself to do something you don't want to do. But how do you do that? What skill is required? There isn't a skill—it's just forcing yourself to do something you don't want to do. And that requires . . . some kind of motivation. Without motivation, you won't be able to force yourself to do anything. So motivation is the key concept—and this is something that's real, that you can actually learn how to do.

3. Focus on motivation. What's your motivation for pursuing the goal or habit? How will you sustain the motivation when you struggle? Have very strong motivations for doing something, and write them down. Commit publicly. When things get tough, remind yourself of your motivation. Focus on it. It'll pull you along—that's more powerful than trying to focus on the push of discipline.

4. Make it easy. Discipline is tough because whatever the task or habit you're trying to do is tough. Instead, make it easy. Remove barriers. Having a hard time exercising? Make it ridiculously easy, by only exercising for 5 minutes. What use is exercising for 5 minutes? You're creating the habit, not getting yourself into shape overnight. The 5 minutes of exercise will have only a tiny impact on your health, but it makes exercise super easy. If you can do that 30 days in a row, you now have an exercise habit. Hate waking up early to go to the gym? Do it at home. Do it during lunch or after work.

5. Focus on enjoyment. It's hard to push yourself—to have discipline—when you hate doing something. So find something enjoyable about the activity. If you don't look forward to exercise, find some good music, or a workout partner who you can have a nice conversation with, or a peaceful setting in nature that is just beautiful. And focus on that enjoyable aspect. Hate doing your paperwork? Find a peaceful sanctuary where you can do the paperwork and enjoy yourself. Maybe have a nice cup of tea or coffee, play some nice music. And focus on the enjoyment.

6. Repeat. You'll almost inevitably slip up sometime, no matter how good you are. Unfortunately, people often take this to mean they don't have discipline, and they just beat themselves up and give up. Well, it's just a bump in the road. Get up, dust yourself off, and get going again. Start from Step 1 and start all over.

Chapter 11

16 Ways to Motivate Yourself When You're in a Slump

By Leo Babauta

Even the most motivated of us—you, me, Tony Robbins—can feel unmotivated at times. In fact, sometimes we get into such a slump that even thinking about making positive changes seems too difficult.

But it's not hopeless: with some small steps, baby ones in fact, you can get started down the road to positive change. Yes, I know, it seems impossible at times. You don't feel like doing anything. I've been there, and in fact I still feel that way from time to time. You're not alone. But I've learned a few ways to break out of a slump, and we'll take a look at those today.

This chapter was inspired by reader Roy C. Carlson, who asked, "I was wondering if you could do a piece on why it can be hard for someone to change direction and start taking control of their life. I have to say I'm in this boat and advice on getting out of my slump would be great."

Roy is just one of many with a slump like that. Again, I feel that way sometimes myself, and in fact sometimes I struggle to motivate myself to exercise—and I'll use that as an example of how to break out of the slump.

When I fall out of exercise, due to illness or injury or disruption from things going on in my life, it's hard to get started again. I don't even feel like thinking about it, some-times. But I've always found a way to break out of that slump, and here are some things I've learned that have helped:

1. One Goal. Whenever I've been in a slump, I've discovered that it's often because I have too much going on in my life. I'm trying to do too much. And it saps my energy and motivation. It's probably the most common mistake that people make: they try to take on too much, try to accomplish too many goals at once. You cannot maintain energy and focus (the two most important things in accomplishing a goal) if you are trying to do two or more goals at once. It's not possible—I've tried it many times. You have to choose one goal, for now, and focus on it completely. I know, that's hard. Still, I speak from experience. You can always do your other goals when you've accomplished your One Goal.

2. Find inspiration. Inspiration, for me, comes from others who have achieved what I want to achieve, or who are currently doing it. I read other blogs, books, magazines. I Google my goal, and read success stories. Zen Habits is just one place for inspiration, not only from me but from many readers who have achieved amazing things.

3. Get excited. This sounds obvious, but most people don't think about it much: if you want to break out of a slump, get yourself excited about a goal. But how can you do that when you don't feel motivated? Well, it starts with inspiration from others (see above), but you have to take that excitement and build on it. For me, I've learned that by talking to my wife about it, and to others, and reading as much about it as possible, and visualizing what it would be like to be successful (seeing the benefits of the goal in my head), I get excited about a goal. Once I've done that, it's just a matter of carrying that energy forward and keeping it going.

4. Build anticipation. This will sound hard, and many people will skip this tip. But it really works. It helped me

quit smoking after many failed attempts. If you find inspiration and want to do a goal, don't start right away. Many of us will get excited and want to start today. That's a mistake. Set a date in the future—a week or two, or even a month—and make that your Start Date. Mark it on the calendar. Get excited about that date. Make it the most important date in your life. In the meantime, start writing out a plan. And do some of the steps below. Because by delaying your start, you are building anticipation, and increasing your focus and energy for your goal.

5. Post your goal. Print out your goal in big words. Make your goal just a few words long, like a mantra ("Exercise 15 mins. Daily"), and post it up on your wall or refrigerator. Post it at home and work. Put it on your computer desktop. You want to have big reminders about your goal, to keep your focus and keep your excitement going. A picture of your goal (like a model with sexy abs, for example) also helps.

6. Commit publicly. None of us likes to look bad in front of others. We will go the extra mile to do something we've said publicly. For example, when I wanted to run my first marathon, I started writing a column about it in my local daily newspaper. The entire island of Guam (pop. 160K) knew about my goal. I couldn't back down, and even though my motivation came and went, I stuck with it and completed it. Now, you don't have to commit to your goal in your daily newspaper, but you can do it with friends and family and co-workers, and you can do it on your blog if you have one. And hold yourself accountable—don't just commit once, but commit to giving progress updates to everyone every week or so.

7. Think about it daily. If you think about your goal every day, it is much more likely to become true. To this end, posting the goal on your wall or computer desktop (as mentioned above) helps a lot. Sending yourself daily reminders also helps. And if you can commit to doing one small thing

to further your goal (even just 5 minutes) every single day, your goal will almost certainly come true.

8. Get support. It's hard to accomplish something alone. When I decided to run my marathon, I had the help of friends and family, and I had a great running community on Guam who encouraged me at 5K races and did long runs with me. When I decided to quit smoking, I joined an online forum and that helped tremendously. And of course, my wife Eva helped every step of the way. I couldn't have done these goals without her, or without the others who supported me. Find your support network, either in the real world or online, or both.

9. Realize that there's an ebb and flow. Motivation is not a constant thing that is always there for you. It comes and goes, and comes and goes again, like the tide. But realize that while it may go away, it doesn't do so permanently. It will come back. Just stick it out and wait for that motivation to come back. In the meantime, read about your goal (see below), ask for help (see below), and do some of the other things listed here until your motivation comes back.

10. Stick with it. Whatever you do, don't give up. Even if you aren't feeling any motivation today, or this week, don't give up. Again, that motivation will come back. Think of your goal as a long journey, and your slump is just a little bump in the road. You can't give up with every little bump. Stay with it for the long term, ride out the ebbs and surf on the flows, and you'll get there.

11. Start small. Really small. If you are having a hard time getting started, it may be because you're thinking too big. If you want to exercise, for example, you may be thinking that you have to do these intense workouts 5 days a week. No—instead, do small, tiny, baby steps. Just do 2 minutes of exercise. I know, that sounds wimpy. But it works. Commit to 2 minutes of exercise for one week. You may want to do more, but just stick to 2 minutes. It's so easy, you can't fail. Do it at

the same time, every day. Just some crunches, 2 pushups, and some jogging in place. Once you've done 2 minutes a day for a week, increase it to 5, and stick with that for a week. In a month, you'll be doing 15–20. Want to wake up early? Don't think about waking at 5 A.M. Instead, think about waking 10 minutes earlier for a week. That's all. Once you've done that, wake 10 minutes earlier than that. Baby steps.

12. Build on small successes. Again, if you start small for a week, you're going to be successful. You can't fail if you start with something ridiculously easy. Who can't exercise for 2 minutes? (If that's you, I apologize.) And you'll feel successful, and good about yourself. Take that successful feeling and build on it, with another baby step. Add 2–3 minutes to your exercise routine, for example. With each step (and each step should last about a week), you will feel even more successful. Make each step really, really small, and you won't fail. After a couple of months, your tiny steps will add up to a lot of progress and a lot of success.

13. Read about it daily. When I lose motivation, I just read a book or blog about my goal. It inspires me and reinvigorates me. For some reason, reading helps motivate and focus you on whatever you're reading about. So read about your goal every day, if you can, especially when you're not feeling motivated.

14. Call for help when your motivation ebbs. Having trouble? Ask for help. Email me. Join an online forum. Get a partner to join you. Call your mom. It doesn't matter who, just tell them your problems, and talking about it will help. Ask them for advice. Ask them to help you overcome your slump. It works.

15. Think about the benefits, not the difficulties. One common problem is that we think about how hard something is. Exercise sounds so hard! Just thinking about it makes you tired. But instead of thinking about how hard something is,

think about what you will get out of it. For example, instead of thinking about how tiring exercise can be, focus on how good you'll feel when you're done, and how you'll be healthier and slimmer over the long run. The benefits of something will help energize you.

16. Squash negative thoughts; replace them with positive ones. Along those lines, it's important to start monitoring your thoughts. Recognize negative self-talk, which is really what's causing your slump. Just spend a few days becoming aware of every negative thought. Then, after a few days, try squashing those negative thoughts like a bug, and then replacing them with a corresponding positive thought. Squash, "This is too hard!" and replace it with, "I can do this! If that wimp Leo can do it, so can I!" It sounds corny, but it works. Really.

Chapter 12

5 Tips For Motivational Recovery

By Eric Hamm

Part of staying motivated is being able to recover when you start to loose your drive. It happens to all of us at one time or another. Sometimes it's just because we're tired and other times we'll find that we lose perspective. Maybe you've just lost your vision of what you are trying to accomplish. Either way, it is greatly important that you have a plan for recovery. A motivational "first aid kit" as it were. Here are 5 tips that always seem to help keep me on track.

1. Get some sleep. There's a good chance that if you are losing your drive you may just be experiencing some form of burn out. If this is the case sleep is the best medicine. You may be thinking, "I get sleep every night. What are you talking about?" But I am talking a full night's sleep. Deep sleep. You may be getting *some* sleep but if you are not consistently getting the kind of sleep your body needs to function at it's best you will eventually start to l ose your edge. Sleep is what your body needs to repair itself from the abuse of the day. Not only that, your "feel good" hormones are replenished when you get a good night's sleep. This is why you may feel much more optimistic after a good night's sleep. So go to bed early, listen to some calming music and try to clear your mind of the stress of the day. But whatever you do, just get it done. You positive, optimistic, motivated mindset depends on it.

2. Get some exercise. We all know that regular exercise is good for our bodies. But it is also one of your greatest assets when it comes to staying motivated. Just like a good night's sleep, regular exercise keeps a steady stream of that "optimistic juice" flowing throughout your mind and body. Chemicals like endorphins are produced when you exercise. These kinds of chemicals help you feel good about yourself and your situation.

Exercise does much more, though. It helps you feel like you are treating your body right. You feel like you've accomplished something good and, over time, you gain strength and energy. And besides all of that, exercising is a great way to clear your head when you are stressed. So make sure to get as much as your mind and body needs to stay driven to your goals.

3. Get away. When all else fails you might just be in need of a healthy escape. Sleep and exercise can be a form of this but physically going somewhere, preferably a place that helps you relax, can be a great way of clearing your head and re-energizing your soul. There may be a great place in the country that you like to go and have time to yourself. Or maybe getting together with family and just hanging out. Just give yourself a break so that when you get back into the swing of things you will have a fresh perspective and, hopefully, a revived spirit of optimism and focus.

4. Look at the alternatives. I find that often times the best medicine is a little shock therapy. In this case it's a matter of seeing what lies in store for you if you decide to give up on your dreams. It can be quite scary if you really take a look at the mediocrity that is in store for those who give up and take the easy road. Look at the average on the street who is just "getting by" and see that this may be you in the near future. Remind yourself that this may be living but it is certainly *not* being alive!

5. Go back to the beginning. Sometimes the problem is just that you have lost the vision that you started with. In the beginning our dreams are very enticing. But then that feeling starts to fade. We quickly forget what our dream looks like. We can't see it, smell it or touch it. Without this picture of what we are striving for we will most certainly lose the drive to seek it out. So it is important to go back to the beginning when you first started your journey. Try to remember exactly *what* you are after. Try to re-paint the picture of your dream with the same brush, with the same thoughts and feelings that you had when you first created this work of art. There's a good chance that you will start to see things that you had forgotten and remember exactly *why* you are seeking these upgrades to your life.

Chapter 13

The Magical Power of Focus

By Leo Babauta

"Always remember, your focus determines your reality."
—Qui-Gon to Anakin, Star Wars Episode I

The quote above, as cheesy as George Lucas's writing often is, contains a nugget of Jedi wisdom that I've repeatedly found to be true.

Your focus determines your reality.

It's something we don't think about much of the time, but give it some consideration now:

• If you wake up in the morning and think about the miserable things you need to do later in the day, you'll have a miserable day. If you wake up and focus instead on what a wonderful gift your life is, you'll have a great day.

• If we let our attention jump from one thing to another, we will have a busy, fractured and probably unproductive day. If we focus entirely on one job, we may lose ourselves in that job, and it will not only be the most productive thing we do all day, but it'll be very enjoyable.

• If we focus on being tired and wanting to veg out in front of the TV, we will get a lot of television watching done. If, however, we focus on being healthy and fit, we will become healthy and fit through exercise and good eating. This may seem simplistic, but it's completely true. This is the magical power of focus.

Let's look at some of the ways you can use focus to improve different aspects of your life.

"All that we are is the result of what we have thought."
—*Buddha*

FOCUS ON A GOAL

In my experience, focus is the most important determination of whether you'll achieve a goal or stick to creating a new habit. Not self-discipline, not rewards, not sheer willpower, not even motivation (also an important ingredient, however). If you can maintain your focus on a goal or habit, you will more often than not achieve that goal or create that habit.

If you can't maintain your focus, you won't achieve the goal, unless it's such an easy goal that it would have happened anyway. It's that simple.

Why does focus matter so much? Let's say you decide you want to declutter your house—that's your goal for this month. So the first day, you're completely focused on this goal, and you get boxes and trash bags and fill them up with junk. The second day, you're still focused, and you fill up a bunch more boxes and you've cleared most of two rooms with progress on another. This goes on for a few more days, with your focus being on this goal, and lots of progress made.

However, let's say that a week into your decluttering, you decide you want to become a runner. You are now focused on running, and not only do you go out to jog for a few days, you buy running clothes and a Nike-equipped iPod and read running blogs and magazines. However, you've lost your focus on decluttering, and soon you aren't doing much of it, because your focus is on running. In fact, you've added more clutter because you've bought all the running equipment and magazines and books.

Meanwhile, I have maintained my focus on decluttering the entire month, and by the end of the month, I have a nice, simplified house. I did it through focus.

This is why I am constantly advocating focusing on only one goal at a time. Having multiple goals spreads out your focus,

and makes it less likely that you'll complete any of the goals. It's possible, but with a diffused focus, it's much more difficult.

Even with only one goal, maintaining focus can be difficult. You need to find ways to keep your focus on that goal. Some good examples that work for me:

• Read about your goal as much as possible, on websites and blogs and in books and magazines.

• Post up reminders on your wall, refrigerator, and computer desktop.

• Send yourself reminders using an online calendar or reminder service.

• Tell as many people as possible about it, and post your progress on your blog.

• Have a time each day to work on the goal, with a reminder in your schedule each day. Maintain your focus on your goal, and you've won half the battle in achieving it.

FOCUS ON NOW

I've written about this before, but focusing on the present can do a lot for you. It helps reduce stress, it helps you enjoy life to the fullest, and it can increase your effectiveness.

Focusing on now, rather than the past ("I can't believe she said that to me!") or the future ("what am I going to say in the darn meeting today?") isn't easy, and takes a lot of practice.

FOCUS ON THE TASK AT HAND

Have you ever completely lost yourself in a task, so that the world around you disappears? You lose track of time and are completely caught up in what you're doing. That's the popular concept of Flow, and it's an important ingredient to finding happiness.

Having work and leisure that gets you in this state of flow will almost undoubtedly lead to happiness. People find greatest enjoyment not when they're passively mindless, but when they're absorbed in a mindful challenge.

How do you get into flow? Well, it takes a bit of practice, but the first step is to find work that you're passionate about. Seriously—this is an extremely important step. Find hobbies that you're passionate about. Turn off the TV—this is the opposite of flow—and get outside and do something that truly engages you.

Next, you need to clear away distractions and focus completely on the task you set before yourself. This is the part that takes a lot of practice. I'll write more about this later.

FOCUS ON THE POSITIVE

One of the key skills I've learned is how to be aware of my negative thoughts, and to replace them with positive thoughts. I learned this through quitting smoking and running—there are many times when you feel like giving up, and if you don't catch these negative thoughts in time, they'll fester and grow until you actually do give up.

Instead, learn to focus on the positive. Think about how great you feel. Think about how other people have done this, and so can you. Think about how good it will feel when you accomplish what you're trying to do.

Also learn to see the positive in just about any situation. This results in happiness, in my experience, as you don't focus on the bad parts of your life, but on the good things. Be thankful for what you've been given.

"We are what we think; as we desire so do we become! By our thoughts, desires, and habits, we either ascend to the full divine dignity of our nature, or we descend to suffer and learn." —J. Todd Ferrier

Chapter 14

10 Ways to Beat the "Can't Get No Satisfaction" Syndrome

By Leo Babauta

Are you feeling like life isn't exciting enough? That maybe you're missing out on something because you just can't get motivated for anything? Turns out you're not alone.

Recently, reader Rachel asked:

"In a population of 6 billion+ people globally, it is hard not to feel like another number. I find life so disenchanting the more I pursue things I though were my dreams. I am at possibly the top university in the world getting my masters to make the world a better place . . . yet I lack the joy and excitement that I should have. If this were just my problem, I would figure this out, but I think so many of us deal with this. We can have so much to be grateful for, and we very well might be grateful . . . however, when the achievement of a dream fails to make us as satisfied as we thought it would, it calls the very credibility of dreaming into question. I appreciate the process of life, one might say . . . Nothing seems to be that exciting though . . . nothing could surprise me anymore. I was wondering if you had any insight on this issue . . . i.e. what I call the "I can't get no satisfaction" syndrome."

What a tough question! How do you get excited about life?

I have to admit that this is not only a common problem, but one of the toughest. I've gone through times in my life

when nothing seemed exciting. Dreams seemed utterly hopeless and useless. Motivation was a hard currency to come by.

So what changed? What got me excited by life?

There's no one answer. What follows is a series of things
that worked for me, in no particular order . . . I should note
that some of these may sound trite, but they actually do work,
for me and for countless others:

1. Make small, positive changes. This is a bit of a paradox.
Making small, positive changes—eating a little healthier, exercising a little, creating some small productive habits, for
example—are an amazing way to get excited about life . . .
but doesn't it take some excitement and motivation to even
get started with these small changes? Yes, a little . . . but not
a lot. If you start small, you don't need a lot of motivation.
Just get going. You'll soon find that just the act of getting
started and doing something will give you some momentum,
and soon you'll be in a positive spiral of changes—one building on the other. When I started doing this in my life, I was
so excited I had to start Zen Habits to share it with the world.

2. Banish negative thinking. Negative thoughts are the
bane of an exciting existence. You can't have all these negative thoughts, and hope to really enjoy life. It's one or the
other—and it's your choice. Do you want to think negative—
I can't do it, this sucks—or do you want to love life and do
amazing things and get excited about everything? It really is
a choice. And it takes awareness—be aware of your thoughts
and when you catch yourself thinking negative, squash the
thought like a bug, and replace it with a positive thought. Seriously, it works. I did this with running and smoking when
I first started, and I was able to successfully start running
and quit smoking. That was more than three years ago, and
I haven't smoked since and I've run three marathons since
then. All because I banished negative thoughts.

3. Look at the wonderful side of things. This is kinda the
flip side of No. 2 above, but I don't care—it's so important I

need to give it its own list item. Yes, that's right—it matters that much: everything around you has a wonderful side, and you just need to look at that to realize how lucky you are. Seriously. My internet went down? That's a wonderful thing: I was more productive than ever before, plus I spent more time with my kids rather than surfing the web. My daughter is throwing a tantrum because she wants a toy her brother is playing with? It's a wonderful opportunity for me to teach her about sharing, to invent some fun new activity we can do together, to spend some time with my kids. My grandfather died? It's a wonderful chance for me to celebrate the great life he led, the influence he had on me and those around me, to learn more about him, to spend time with friends and family, to reflect on the preciousness of life.

4. Exercise. Not everyone is a fan of exercise, but I can tell you firsthand that it can work miracles. While many people do it to improve their appearance, there's so much more to exercise—it can be incredibly fun while you're doing it (if you do it right), you feel healthy and energetic, you can get a fresh insight into your life and life in general. When I exercise, I feel so much better than those days when I don't. It gives me new ideas, time to contemplate, time to spend with my sister (who is my friend and running partner). Start with just 10 minutes a day and you'll see how much it can energize your life.

5. Appreciate loved ones. It's not a secret that I'm a big fan of spending time with my family. It's my No. 1 favorite pastime. And for good reason: when I do so, I love life so much more. Even just laying on the couch reading together, or renting a movie and eating take-out food, or walking along the beach together, or cracking jokes with each other—it really makes life so much better. Take the time to appreciate your loved ones, and if you haven't spent time with them lately, do so today if you can! At the very least, give your loved ones a call or send a nice email.

6. Pursue a passion. This was a life-changer for me. For many years, I was too afraid or too pessimistic to pursue my passion (writing) seriously. In January 2007, I started Zen Habits as a way to pursue that passion, and it was one of the best decisions of my life (my wife and children being the others). Even if I didn't make money from blogging, I'd love it and it would be worth doing just for the energy it infuses into my life. Whatever your passion, pursue it with energy. If you don't know what that passion is, you need to start exploring and trying new things—it could take awhile, but it's worth the effort.

7. Talk and work with other excited people. Boy, this is really a great one. I wish someone had told me about this a decade ago. I've worked with competent people before, but looking back on it, often they were jaded or cynical or negative in some way. And these negative, bored people would have an effect on my attitude. But the times when I've worked with people who are excited about what they do . . . well, I'd get excited too. Even today, when I basically work alone, I collaborate with other great bloggers, with others on some cool projects . . . and I seek out people who get excited about what they do. It's fun to work with them, and it makes things much more exciting.

8. Take time to recharge. Sometimes you just feel drained, and you can't get excited about anything. This is a good time to take a break if you can, to get out of your usual setting and your usual routine. You don't have to go to the Caribbean or Guam (although if you can, that's great) . . . just get out into nature, reflect on life, realize how wonderful it is, do some journaling or sketching, create, have fun, relax, do nothing. When you're done, you'll feel much better about everything, and come at things with a fresh perspective.

9. Get great feedback. One of the things I love about blogging at Zen Habits is the amazing feedback and encouragement I get from my readers. It has made blogging a

joy, and the feedback I get has helped me to improve every step of the way. I get excited about what I do because I love the feedback—both the praise and the constructive criticism. I don't love the hateful comments, but those are rare. While not everyone will become a blogger, it's great if you can get some great feedback from people—coworkers, peers, friends and family, clients and customers. The more, the better. When you get negative feedback, use it to get better. When you get praise, bask in it and be grateful.

10. Help others. I don't pretend that I'm the world's greatest philanthropist, but often I get emails and comments from people who have improved their lives from what I've done. And the feeling I get from comments like this is unbelievable. I am incredibly grateful to be able to help others, even in a small way, and I highly recommend it to everyone. Even if your main job isn't dedicated to helping others, find spare time to do volunteer charity work or find ways to do nice things to help your loved ones. It'll make life so much better.

Chapter 15

30 Incredible Places to Turn When You Need Inspiration

By Leo Babauta

"Your time is limited, so don't waste it living someone else's life. Don't be trapped by dogma—which is living with the results of other people's thinking. Don't let the noise of other's opinions drown out your own inner voice. And most important, have the courage to follow your heart and intuition. They somehow already know what you truly want to become. Everything else is secondary." —Steve Jobs

Have you ever just run out of inspiration and didn't know where to turn? Of course you have—we all have. I face this situation at least once a week.

And while I've written about some of my favorite sources of inspiration before, I decided to turn to all of you for ideas. I asked the question on Twitter: Where do you turn to when you need inspiration?

The responses were overwhelming. I couldn't reprint all of them, but I picked a handful of my favorites (I liked many more than the ones below). Here they are—30 great sources of inspiration, thanks to my friends on Twitter:

1. Be open at all times—the best inspiration finds you. (@ecyaj)

2. The Bible. (@yclept_john, @flaimster, @sdatexas, @PreacherNorm, @kylemaxwell)

3. Blogs like Zen Habits, Think Simple Now, Dumb Little Man. (@GentleLiving, @Imokon, and others)

4. Poetry. (@Eusebius)

5. When overwhelmed with thinking, I just need to clear everything out and focus. (@Imokon)

6. Inner film. I close my eyes and start a movie projector in my head, and wait for the projected film to start. It always works. (@montjo)

7. Pull out an Ansel Adams or Walker Evans book. Instant inspiration! (@OoffAhh)

8. Music (@larudden, @Nexxion, and others) From @DannyLamas: "Music, always. Whether it's motivational or creative inspiration." From @ndsizemore: "Quick inspiration, for me, often comes from my music collection."

9. Large doses of silence. (@schizoidnix) Also, from @laughsoutloud: "I take the time to get quiet. Then it all flows." And from @SpiritChaser1 26: "I quiet my mind and The Universe usually starts to show me exactly what I need to see throughout the day."

10. I look within. (@ksweeney253)

11. The ocean. (@Xyc0)

12. Nature. (@cafegurl) From @Maggie2Day: "For true inspiration I turn to nature . . . always straightens me out if I am opened to go straight." From @africankelli: "Sunrise hikes, in particular."

13. For inspiration I go outside for a walk. (@hiwendee) From @ninabarnard: "I go outside and walk, breathe deep, notice all colors, sounds, smells and think of what I'm grateful for."

14. Thumb through magazines at bookstore. (@hiwendee)

15. Mountains. Any mountains. (@silverbenz)

16. A shower. (@juanmab)

17. Look at the sky and think big! (@crackpat)

18. Call a friend to brainstorm. (@marriedwluggage)

19. Books: library, store, my bookshelf. Grab a latte and cruise Barnes & Noble. (@sarahgbennett)

20. The present. Enjoying the now. (@shaunl17)

21. When I read something on the web that inspires me (usually from blogs), I save in delicious. I go there when I need inspiration. (@noodlesome)

22. Jack Canfield's The Success Principles. (@Fred0828)

23. My friends and family! (@goopster24)

24. One-minute stillness meditation by Stacy Mayo. (@annijm)

25. This will sound new-agey, but I like to sit there and let the lack of inspiration be until it dissolves. (@acordaamor)

26. Steve Jobs' Stanford speech. (@ctolsen)

27. I run, alone. (@jsaldiva)

28. I find people who do things that seem impossible and try to figure out how they did them. Their quotes are backed by their story. (@saxmanmike)

29. TED.com inspirational talks. (@rbadr)

30. And (cue drumroll) . . . a cool new Zen Habits poster! (From the gorgeous Goddess Leonie, who has promised to bake me cupcakes. Yumm.)

Chapter 16

How To Deal With Negative Feedback

By Eric Hamm

As human beings, we are affected by the feedback we receive from those around us. Whether good, bad or neutral, the words we hear and the tone in which they are seasoned, can have a powerful impact on how we feel about ourselves and how we see the world around us. From the time we first take notice of this double edge we call the tongue, we are keenly aware of its sting as well as its ability to uplift the somber soul.

FEELING THE STING OF A VERBAL ATTACK

I recently received an email from one of my websites that was anything but positive in nature. I was basically told, by a total stranger that had just laid eyes on my site for the very first time, that I was a worthless piece of @#$%. This person seemed to go to great lengths to tare me down as quickly and effectively as possible. I had been having quite a tough week and this was just one more stone that had met its intended target.

I started to reply, trying to stay calm and not be a jerk right back, but I was having a hard time not getting defensive. So I got Liz to read the email and asked her opinion. The second she had finished reading the words of this viscous verbal assault, she looked at me and said, "Eric, why would you even give this person two seconds of your time? Just delete it and move on." Realizing the foolishness of trying to defend myself to someone who had no intention of having a two way conversation, I deleted the email and tried my best to forget about it.

Later that day, while walking our dogs, Liz and I discussed the situation. She admitted that it was easy for her to tell me to forget about it, but that if it had been directed at her, it most certainly would have bothered her, but that paying attention to that kind of feedback will do nothing but bring you down. That absolutely *no good* could ever come from responding to the kind of hate that was in that email. I agreed and I moved on.

THE EFFECT OF FEEDBACK

I don't know about you, but when I have a couple of days that are filled with nothing but positive reinforcement and encouragement, I can't help but feel light on my feet. I have more energy, get more done and tend to be a more positive person. But this can easily be brought to a screeching halt if the right words are used. Something like that email I described above can really take the wind out of my sales if I let it. I like for people to like me and I enjoy sharing positive experiences, not baring the brunt of someone else's bad day. I want to help people when they are in need, not get stepped on when things don't go their way.

There's a saying, "Water off a duck's back." This usually pertains to a situation where an individual is criticized, but not affected by it. Somehow this person is able to let the negativity just roll right off their hypothetical back. This is rare and often times falsely mentioned. We are *very* effected by feedback from others and it is near impossible to completely disregard the different colored sound waves that find their way to our acute audible sensors. So let's not kid ourselves. We generally *do* care what others think about us and both positive *and* negative feedback will usually have at least *some* effect on us. The question isn't, "How can we ignore certain sound waves?" But instead, "How can we properly channel the different tones that take aim at us?" Just like certain martial arts may teach, it is better to go with the force of the attacking blow and use its energy to benefit yourself, than it is to try and fight it, or in many cases, try and ignore it.

How To Stop Letting People Make Or Break Your Life

So you're like me in that your mindset, motivation and productivity arc sometimes dictated by the feedback of the people around you. You're sick of working hard to build up momentum, only to be taken out at the knees by a barrage of negativity.

Let's stop handing over the keys to other people's opinions and bring stability to our personal perspective of ourselves.

Tip #1: Determine the usefulness of the negative feedback.

As we all know, just because something is negative doesn't mean it is wrong and/or can't be turned into a positive. When we first receive feedback that threatens to bring us down we need to ask ourselves if there is anything useful we can take from it. Are we doing something wrong? Can we learn from this to improve our tomorrow? If there is merit to the comment and we can learn from it, we should determine the lesson, learn it and then go about our business. But if it turns out to be a difference of opinion or just negativity for the sake of negativity, we must see it for what it is (someone esle's problem) and move on.

Tip #2: Beware of the dangerous Half-Truth

When others attempt to bring us down, they often do so by using the good old half-truth. They throw in *just* enough truth to get us second guessing ourselves and then naturally becoming defensive.

Think about it. When you have received negative feedback, was it the completely false statements that effected you most, or those that had a bit of truth sprinkled in with the lies? When there is some truth involved, we naturally pay attention and often try and pick through the statement to figure out what exactly needs to be done. We think, "Well, that one part is true and I *kind of* do that thing they pointed out, but the way they spin the idea is completely false."

The problem with this is that we can find ourselves stuck in a pointless cycle of trying to reason out what may just be a bunch of false information that had no intention of constructively criticizing us. We spin our wheels attempting to effectively determine a defense, when no defense is needed or even advisable. This is often a complete waste of time. So how do we deal with these deceivingly destructive accusations without lowering our standards and losing valuable time? It's quite simple, actually. We just need to look at the *entire* statement and not just the individual points. Let's say you own a bakery and specialize in blueberry muffins. One day the owner of the bakery across the street comes in and says,"You sell your muffins for less than I do. (*truth*) From what I can tell, you've found a way to get the same ingredients for less than I can get them (*truth*) and have come up with a way to make your muffins in half the time (*truth*). Way to go! You've just brought down the standards of the muffin making industry!" (*false*)

OK, so this guy obviously had it in for you from the get go, but he *did* lay down a bunch of truths. Up until the very end, he was describing your actions with great detail. But he then managed to spin those facts into one final false accusation. Now you're thinking, "Is it possible that my actions are wrong in some way? Should I re-think the way I'm doing things?" We need to realize that a statement is either true or false. Their may be some truths and some lies mixed in, but the entire statement is saying something specific, and it is the point that it's trying to make that is either true or false. So if we were to look at this competitor's statement as either true or false, we could clearly see it as false. But fall into the trap of picking it apart and we only confuse ourselves with conflicting information.

Another trick is to remove the false parts of the statement and then repeat what's left, but in a positive tone. Let's picture an appreciative customer who's eating one of your delicious blueberry muffins and positively saying the exact statement, minus the last bit of lies. "You sell your muffins for less than the baker across the street. From what I can tell, you've found a way to get the same ingredients for less than he can get them and have come up with a way to make your muffins in half the time. Way to go!" Same statement, minus the lies, with a positive tone. *Completely* different statement! So remember that it's often times not the words being said, but the intentions behind them that determine their tone. If changing the intentions changes the tone, then you're most likely dealing with a mere opinion and not a fact of any kind.

Tip #3: Determine who you will listen to

As much as that email was hurtful with its malicious message, the author in no way fit the profile of an individual I would ever care to absorb opinion. It's absolutely crucial that we know exactly what kind of person we care to mind and therefore what type of individual we will pay *no* mind.

For myself, I will always at least hear out family and friends. This is, for the most part, a given. But even here we need to be cautious. Be sure this loved one has proper perspective to be paying you thought. Even a friend isn't always going to give good advice.

But what about mere acquaintances or even total strangers? Some great advice has been given to me by strangers, so their lack of relationship to you should never keep you from learning from their insight. It then comes down to their values, their mindset when sharing the thought and what they have to gain by your reaction to the comment.

It was obvious to me that the author of this email was not acting from a healthy set of values. That this individual was not in a good mindset when they typed the hateful words and that the only thing they had to gain from my reaction was a sense of twisted satisfaction that they had knocked me down a notch. It was obvious to me that this person did *not* hold an opinion that I needed to be mindful of. And Once I realized this, it made it much easier to disregard them as someone having a bad day and frankly, not my concern.

Tip #4: Accept your imperfections

We may be fully aware that we are not perfect people, but it can still sting when that imperfection is pointed out by another. We try so hard to think things through and cover all the bases, but sometimes we drop the ball. When this occurs and you get some flack for it, lean to take it in stride. Quite often I find myself over focusing on a pointed out imperfection, trying to determine what went wrong and what I could have done differently. This in itself can be a good thing, a way to learn from our mistakes, but once we find ourselves feeling discouraged as a result, we need to step back and accept the fact that *everyone* makes mistakes. The more comfortable you are with the fact that you're going to trip up from time to time, the quicker you'll bounce back when others make your imperfections known.

Tip #5: Take a breather

The worst thing you can do when dealing with negative feedback is let your pride get involved. You may want to lash out at someone or stoop down to their level. This is *never* a good thing. You either continue a useless conversation or stoke the flames of a fire that only burns as long as two continue to tango.

Instead of reacting (and quite possibly over-reacting), sleep on it. Give yourself some time to get away from the situation and even forget about it for a bit. Let your subconscious chew on it for a while and see what it thinks. The following day you can re-visit the issue and determine your course of action with a much greater chance of choosing wisely. You may decide like I did that no response is necessary. Or that becoming defensive will serve no purpose. Whichever rout you choose, you'll be doing so from a level perspective and not an in-the-moment reaction that might very well create more problems than you started out with.

Tip #6: Build momentum regardless of reaction

Just as much as we should not let negative feedback knock us down, we need to be cautious about how much we rely on the positive to push us forward. There's nothing wrong with riding the waves of encouragement, but if this is the foundation we chose to build our future success, we will see our personal development crumble, time and time again. Our motivation should come from knowing we are moving in the the right direction and that we are unwilling to settle for less than awesome. We can enjoy the pats on the back when they come, but our identity needs to be formed from a foundation independent of those around us.

FINAL THOUGHTS

The bottom line is that as long as we are striving to better our lives as well as those around us, we should never fear the negativity that will inevitably come our way. Some will be true and some, half-true, but none should make us feel any less capable than before. Learn to properly filter this feedback and you will always maintain your motivation and proper piece of mind.

Chapter 17

How to Doggedly Pursue Your Dreams in the Face of Naysayers

By Leo Babauta

What do you do if you have a dream, but everyone around you keeps telling you to be more realistic and to give up the dream? What if they want you to pursue a more "sensible" and traditional career route?

You ignore them. You shut out the naysayers, and you stay focused on your dream.

It's the only way. Because in our lives, we will always have naysayers, we will always have negative people, and if we listen to them, we will never pursue our dreams.

Today we'll look at how to do that, and to make those dreams a reality.

Reader Valerie asked me recently:

"I'm barely 17 (turning 18 next February), and I have set goals for my life. But in the world that we live in, where everyone's encouraged to get a steady job, find someone to settle down with, and have a family, I rarely find support for my "crazy" dreams. I want to live in Hong Kong, work in the fashion industry, and I refuse to get married before I turn 30, if I even find someone to marry."

I know that my goals and dreams are completely in my grasp, but with all these speeches about "the real world" that people my age hear constantly, I tend to doubt myself a lot. How can I stay true to myself and stay motivated?

Look at Valerie: she has a dream, and she's ready to take the plunge, to take a risk, to change her life just to make that dream come true. She knows what she wants, she has a plan, she's willing to do more than most of us are willing to do to get what she wants.

And yet, she has doubts, because dreams such as hers are not considered realistic. Those doubts, my friends, are what will stop any of us from achieving our dreams.

DOUBTS ARE THE ENEMY

We all have doubts, and they're unavoidable. And sometimes, it's good to be realistic, because you need to be able to analyze whether a dream is achievable or not.

But if the only thing stopping you is fears and doubts, and not some insurmountable obstacle, then you need to banish those fears and doubts.

Why? Because a doubt, as innocuous as it may seem at first, has a way of creeping its way into your subconscious, into the depths of your heart, like some kind of black and evil creature that has infiltrated your body. The doubt lingers at the back of your head, without you being aware of it, and will eventually conquer your dreams if you let it.

And when this happens, the doubt is more powerful than you realize. When you are making the tough decisions, like whether to apply for college or to go off to Hong Kong and pursue your dreams, your dreams will lose out, because of that doubt in the back of your head. When you think about yourself, your self-image will not be of that person you want to be, but the person that others want you to be.

Doubts will keep you in a job you hate, just because you're afraid to go do what you really want to do. Doubts will keep you with a person who abuses you, because you don't think you deserve better.

HOW TO BANISH DOUBTS IN THREE STEPS

As doubts are so insidious, how do you beat them? It's three simple steps, but each one is a bit more difficult than they sound:

1. Become aware. Doubt gets its power mostly because it is in our subconscious, and we're not aware of the effects it has on us. Instead, we have to bring it to the forefront of our minds. And that means concentrating on our thoughts, and trying to search out those doubts and negative thoughts as they come up. The ones that say, "Maybe I can't do this. Maybe it's not realistic." If you make a conscious effort to be aware of these doubts, you can catch them and beat them.

2. Squash the doubt. Once you've become aware of the doubt, imagine that the doubt is an ugly little bug. Now step on it, and squash it with the bottom of your shoe. Not literally, of course, but in your mind. Exterminate it. Do not let it live and spread!

3. Replace it with something positive. Now that you've squashed the doubt, replace it with positive thoughts. It sounds corny, but trust me, this works: think to yourself, "I can do this! Others have done it, and so can I! Nothing will stop me." Or something along those lines, appropriate to whatever it is you're doing. You have to continue to be vigilant, and be aware of your doubts before they stop you cold in your tracks. This is a constant process as you pursue your dreams, not a one-time thing.

Doubts, like insects, will continue to come back, even after you've killed the first wave or two. You can't let them thrive and overcome you.

WHAT TO DO ABOUT NAYSAYERS

So what about those external negative factors—the naysayers? Those friends and family and people in authority who tell you to stop dreaming, to be realistic, to take a more traditional path? Those who tell you that you can't do something?

You have to learn to block them out. Or, if you have a contrarian streak in you, learn to let those naysayers fuel your determination—make it your desire to prove the naysayers wrong! How do you block out naysayers? The same way you block out doubts and negative thoughts in your own head: you squash them. OK, don't literally squash another person. But when they say something negative, or something that is likely to cause doubts in your head, take that thought (in your head) and squash it. Then replace it with something positive.

If someone is constantly bringing you down and constantly making you feel like you can't do something, you might consider removing them from your life. This sounds drastic, and it can be, but the truth is that having a life full of negative people will drag you down to their level, and stop you from doing what you want to do. I'm not saying you should get a divorce or never see your mother again (if they're the naysayers), but I am saying that you should pick your friends carefully.

Instead, surround yourself with positive, encouraging people. If you have friends like that, you can do anything.

HOW TO TAKE THE PLUNGE

So you've blocked out the naysayers, you've learned to become aware of your doubts and to squash them . . . and you're ready to pursue your dreams.

But you're afraid to take the plunge.

It can be very helpful to do a lot of research and to carefully plan your plunge. But once you've done that research and planning, you still have to take the plunge. How do you do that?

Imagine that you need to swim out to a boat on a lake, and you're standing on the dock, looking down at the icy cold water. You are afraid to dive into that water, but you know you need to take that plunge to get to your boat. So how do you do it? Do you go in one toe at a time? Do you stand there for awhile, waiting for the right moment? Do you wait for someone to give you a push?

No. You have to just do it—just dive in! You've already done all the thinking you need to do. Just dive in.

Once you're in, it'll be freezing, but you're in. You now have no choice but to swim to the boat. And once you've gotten to the boat, you'll be glad you took that plunge.

That's how it is with your dreams. You can't wait for the right moment to come along, or for someone to give you a push, or for the lake to heat up. Just dive right in!

Once you're in, you're committed, and you have to go for it. You don't want to turn back once you've taken the plunge. Now you're more likely to achieve your dreams.

So plan it out, do your research . . . but when you're ready, just dive right in. And don't look back.

HOW TO STAY MOTIVATED

How do you keep your motivation levels high in the face of adversity and obstacles that are sure to come up? Motivation goes up and down, and comes in waves. It's impossible to keep it high all the time.

Here are a few suggestions:

1. Keep the end in mind. Have a clear picture in your head of exactly how you want your dream to turn out in the end. Know where you'll be, what it'll look like, how it will feel. Know exactly what needs to happen for your dream to be a

success—how will you know you've arrived? Keep this clear picture in your head as much as possible.

2. Stay focused. Don't get distracted by other goals or pursuits. If you are tempted to pursue other dreams, do so only with the awareness that you are abandoning your current dream, at least for now. If you don't want to do that, then fight off the temptation of those other pursuits. For now, just stick with this one goal.

3. Get inspired. Who else is achieving this dream, or other dreams? Read about them, talk to them, email them. Go to websites that inspire you. Read books that inspire you. Inspiration is one of the keys to achieving any dream.

4. Celebrate any success. Anything, however small, that you achieve is a cause for joyous celebration. Really. If you're writing a novel, and you've created a great character sketch, celebrate! If you've written your first few paragraphs, celebrate! Your dream will be achieved in baby steps, not in leaps and bounds. Every step is a cause for celebration . . . with enough steps, you'll get there. i

Chapter 18

Achieve Your Dreams Despite Pressures of Work and Family

By Leo Babauta

Do you have dreams you want to pursue, but never seem to have the time because of the twin demands of work and family?

Recently a reader asked:

"I will appreciate if you could post some perspective on lifestyle of people who work in office with lot of peer pressure, pressure from management and juggling between professional, family and personal life. How to make your dreams come true in such kind of environment."

An excellent question, and one that many of us grapple with. I have six kids, and I know what it's like to juggle a hectic work life with a hectic family life. It wasn't long ago that I was trying to make my dreams come true with the twin pressures of work and family bearing down upon me, and I tried many things to overcome this barrier.

So what's the quick answer? There isn't one. It takes hard work. But the most important two factors are:

1. It has to be something you're excited and passionate about; and

2. You have to make it a top priority, and structure your day so that it really is a priority. Let's go into more depth for each of these two factors.

WORK ON SOMETHING YOU'RE EXCITED AND PASSIONATE ABOUT

This step might seem a bit trite or obvious but it's crucial, and I think it's something many people don't think enough about.

Often people think they want to do something, but perhaps it's just something they think would be nice to do . . . not something they're really passionate about. If you're passionate about something, you can't wait to do it, and you'll clear your schedule and make the time to do it. You'll find a way, and when you're doing it, you're excited and happy (and maybe even a little obsessed).

Really think about whether you're excited about your goals or dreams . . . if not, you might need to look for new dreams.

If you are excited, and you're really working hard to pursue the dreams because of this excitement, move on to the next step!

MAKING YOUR DREAMS A PRIORITY

So how do you go from being excited about it to actually doing it? By making your dream your top priority.

That means every day, when you wake up, decide what you're going to do to make that dream a reality. Then do that task first thing in the day, before even checking email. If you can't do it first thing, schedule time for it. If it's a priority, you'll make the time.

But what about work and family? Obviously those are also priorities, so you'll have to schedule time for all three. That might mean cutting back on the work you do, or watching less TV, or doing less Internet surfing or reading, or spending less time on email. Place limits on these routine-type activities, so that you can find the time to work on your dreams.

You might consider waking up earlier, or working late at night when your family is asleep. You might go in to work early so you'll have some quiet time to work on your dreams, or leave early and work on your dreams right after work, or work on your dreams during lunchtime.

You can make the time, if you make it a priority.

TAKE ACTION

It's also important, of course, to take action—you can't just schedule the time. You have to wake up from dreaming and actually get to the doing!

Again, make the action to move closer to your dream the first action you take each day, if at all possible. That way it won't get pushed back to the end of the day, and then to the next day, and so on. Don't let the dream tasks be pushed back!

Try to take action every single day on your dreams. Small steps add up over time.

ENJOY THE JOURNEY

Most of all, enjoy yourself. If you hate what you're doing, you won't do it for long. But if you really enjoy the activity, you won't be able to wait—you'll want to do it right now.

Whether your dream is writing a book or starting a new business or creating your own blog or taking photography or pursuing a graduate degree . . . don't always keep your eye on the destination. Enjoy the journey, right here, right now, and appreciate what a gift it is to be able to follow your dreams.

Chapter 19

Why You Should Celebrate Your Mistakes

By Leo Babauta

When you make a mistake, big or small, cherish it like it's the most precious thing in the world. Because in some ways, it is.

Most of us feel bad when we make mistakes, beat ourselves up about it, feel like failures, get mad at ourselves.

And that's only natural: most of us have been taught from a young age that mistakes are bad, that we should try to avoid mistakes. We've been scolded when we make mistakes—at home, school and work. Maybe not always, but probably enough times to make feeling bad about mistakes an unconscious reaction.

Yet without mistakes, we could not learn or grow.

If you think about it that way, mistakes should be cherished and celebrated for being one of the most amazing things in the world: they make learning possible, they make growth and improvement possible.

By trial and error—trying things, making mistakes, and learning from those mistakes—we have figured out how to make electric light, to paint the ceiling of the Sistine Chapel, to fly.

Mistakes make walking possible for the smallest toddler, make speech possible, make works of genius possible.

Think about how we learn: we don't just consume information about something and instantly know it or know how to do it. You don't just read about painting, or writing, or computer programming, or baking, or playing the piano, and know how to do them right away.

Instead, you get information about something, from reading or from another person or from observing usually . . . then you construct a model in your mind . . . then you test it out by trying it in the real world . . . then you make mistakes . . . then you revise the model based on the results of your real-world experimentation . . . and repeat, making mistakes, learning from those mistakes, until you've pretty much learned how to do something.

That's how we learn as babies and toddlers, and how we learn as adults. Trial and error, learning something new from each error.

Mistakes are how we learn to do something new—because if you succeed at something, it's probably something you already knew how to do. You haven't really grown much from that success—at most it's the last step on your journey, not the whole journey. Most of the journey was made up of mistakes, if it's a good journey.

So if you value learning, if you value growing and improving, then you should value mistakes. They are amazing things that make a world of brilliance possible.

Celebrate your mistakes. Cherish them. Smile.

Chapter 20

How to Actually Execute Your To-do List

By Leo Babauta

Have you gotten good at organizing your tasks in a to-do list, but have trouble actually executing them? You're not alone.

Getting things on your to-do list actually done is difficult because it's really a collection of habits that most people don't think about. Today, we'll look at addressing those issues that stop you from doing things, and the habits needed to overcome those issues.

This chapter was prompted when reader BJ Thunderstone recently asked a great question:

"A lot of productivity systems such as Getting Things Done by David Allen or Do It Tomorrow by Mark Forster concern themselves with writing lists of things to do. This skill is easy to learn.But what if the problem isn't making lists, but executing your plan? What if you write "Get X, Y and Z done" and then you can't make yourself do any of these things?"

I think that many people have a problem not with making to-do lists—but with executing what is written on these lists.

B.J. went on to list some of the reasons he and others have a problem getting things done. Let's address them one by one.

"I FEEL RESISTANCE WHEN STARTING WORK ON SOMETHING."

First of all, it's good to analyze your resistance, which is something we don't do often. Why don't you want to start on something? Identifying the problem can help lead to the solution.

Having said that, there are a couple of suggestions that could help:

• Tiny chunk. Tell yourself you only have to do 5 minutes of work on it. That small amount of work is less intimidating.

• Just start. Once you get going, it's much easier to keep going. So tell yourself that all you have to do is start. I like to compare this to my philosophy of running: instead of worrying about having to do the whole run, I tell myself that I just have to lace up my shoes and get out the door. After that, it's really easy. Do the same thing with any task—just fire up your program, and do the first few actions (i.e. start typing). It gets easier after that point.

• Reward yourself. Don't let yourself check email (or whatever reward works for you—something that you need to do every day) until you do at least 10 minutes (or 15 or 20, it doesn't matter) on the task. Set a timer. Once your 10 minutes is up, set another timer for 5 minutes and do email. Then repeat.

• Get excited about it. This is actually a tip that helps with any of these points. If you are excited about doing something, you will not hesitate to do it. For example, I loved this topic suggestion, and I was excited about writing it. As soon as I had the chance, I sat down to write it and only took one break. But how do you get excited about a task? Try to find something exciting about it. Will it bring you revenue? What can you do with that revenue? Will it bring you new clients, new opportunities, new recognition? If you can't find anything exciting about a task, consider whether it's really important or not—and if not, find a way to not do it. Sometimes eliminating (or delegating or delaying) the task is the best option.

"I AM TERRIFIED OF CERTAIN TASKS, OR OF WORKING ON CERTAIN PROJECTS."

There are usually a few reasons those tasks or projects terrify you:

1. They are too intimidating in size or scope. To combat this, break it down into tinier chunks—actually, just the first tiny chunk (as David Allen tells us to do in GTD). It's intimidating to do a task like "Create report on X" or "Make a yearly plan for Z." But if you just need to do the first physical action, which might be, "Call Frank for figures on X" or "Make a list of 10 things we should accomplish this year," it's much easier to tackle and less intimidating.

2. You don't really know how to do it. If you haven't done something a million times before, it is unfamiliar and unknown to you. And we are all terrified of that. The solution? First, get more information—learn as much as you can about it. That might require some research on the Internet, or talking to someone who's done it before, or reading a book, or taking a class. Whatever you need to do, make the unknown become the known. Second, practice it as much as possible. Once you've learned how to do something, you need to practice it to become good at it. Don't practice the whole thing— practice individual skills required to do a task or project, one at a time, until you're good at those skills. Once you've mastered them, it will no longer be terrifying.

3. You are focusing on negative aspects. You might be focusing on how hard something is, or on all the obstacles. Try looking at the positive aspects instead. Focus on what a great opportunity this project represents . . . an opportunity to learn, to get better at something, to make more money, to

work on a relationship, to gain some long-term recognition, to improve your advancement opportunities. This is similar to the "get excited about it" item in the previous section. If you look at the opportunities, not the problems, you will be less terrified and more likely to want to do it.

"I START, BUT I GET DISTRACTED AND NEVER FINISH."

If you start, you've already made a big step towards finishing. Now you just need to work on the distractions. My suggestions won't be popular, but they work:

• Small tasks. I mentioned this above, but it's really important to repeat here. If you are getting distracted, it may be because you are working too long on a single task or project. To remain focused, do only a small task—you are more likely to stay on task. If the task takes a long time, focus on only doing 15–20 minutes of it.

• Single-task. Don't allow yourself to do multiple tasks at the same time. Just do the one task before you. If you tend to do email, IM, surf the web, read your RSS feeds, talk on the phone and all of that while doing a task, you will inevitably be distracted from a task. Do one task at a time. If you feel yourself being pulled from the task, stop yourself. And bring yourself back.

• Unplug. The biggest distractions come from connectivity. Email, feeds, IM, Twitter, phones. Unplug from these connections while you're working on your single task. This is always an unpopular suggestion, but before you reject it, give it a try. Turn everything off, and try to focus on one task. You'll get a lot more done, I guarantee you. Right now, I'm writing this while disconnected from the Internet. It's much easier to concentrate.

• Clear your desk. Distractions can come from visual clutter. It can be worth it to clear everything off your desk (see 3 Steps to a Permanently Clear Desk). Also clear your walls and your computer desktop, and only work on one program at a time if possible.

• Focus. Once your desk is clear and you unplug, and you're working on that single task, really put all of your concentration on it. Pour your energies into that task, and see if you can get it done quickly. You might even get lost in it, and achieve that highly touted (deservedly so) state of mind known as "flow."

• Take breaks. It can help you to focus for a short amount of time on a single task, and use a time to help you focus, and then to take a break. This allows you to reboot your brain. Then, get back to work and focus on the next task.

"I OFTEN DON'T FEEL LIKE DOING ANY WORK AT ALL. THE IDEA OF WORK SEEMS HORRIBLE AND I NEVER START DOING ANYTHING."

I know this feeling well. It plagues us all, and there's no one good answer. However, here are some suggestions:

• Groom yourself. If you work from home, take a shower. Often the act of grooming ourselves can make us feel much better.

• Take a walk. I find that a little walk can get my blood pumping, refresh my mind, and allow me to think about what I really want to do today. It might not be what you need, but it's worth a shot.

• Exercise. Similarly, exercise can make you feel great. A jog in the park, a short strength workout, some pilates, or meditation . . . these things get your mood up and get you feeling productive and happy. Try it out—you might feel more like doing stuff when you're done.

• Again, think of opportunities. Think about tomorrow— not tomorrow as in the distant future, but tomorrow as in the day after today. Imagine yourself looking back on today from tomorrow. Will you be glad you laid around? Or would you be happier if you did something, and took advantage of the opportunities in front of you today? It's useful to think in terms of your future self—because what we do today will open up opportunities and new roads for tomorrow's us.

• Baby steps. Don't think in terms of having to tackle an entire work day, or an entire list of stuff to do. That's overwhelming. Just think of doing one thing. That's all you have to do—just that one thing. Make it something small and easy, and ideally something fun and rewarding. Focus on that easy task. Once you get started, you might be more willing to do another thing. Then another.

• Find fun stuff to do. If you just have boring or unpleasant things to do, you won't feel like doing them. Instead, change your path for today—see if you can find something that's fun or exciting, but still moves you forward on a project or goal. That might be what you need to get you jump-started to do other stuff—or you might instead only spend the day doing only fun stuff (as long as it moves you forward—don't just play solitaire or WoW).

• Commit thyself. If motivation is your problem, commit yourself to making some progress with a goal or project today, or every day this week—tell all your family and friends, write it in your blog, or join the Zen Habits forum—it's a great motivator. Then hold yourself accountable by reporting to others what you did today.

• Rewards. Tell yourself that if you just do that first task, you'll get a nice ice cream sundae. Or that you can buy a book, or DVD. Whatever your reward, use it to motivate yourself to just get started. Then let the rest flow from there.

"I MAKE A LIST OF THINGS TO DO THE NEXT DAY . . . AND ON THAT DAY, I WAKE UP LOOKING FORWARD TO A BAD DAY, FULL OF UNPLEASANT TASKS, I DON'T FEEL LIKE DOING ANYTHING FROM THE LIST."

Two things to say here:

1. Overload. The most probable reason is that you're overloading yourself. People tend to pile too much on themselves for a single day, overestimating how much they can actually do. Get into the habit of choosing only three Most Important Tasks to do for the day, and do them early in the day (at least two of them before email). If you only have three things to do, it's not overwhelming. You'll probably have some smaller things to do later, but write those down under a "batch process" heading, and do those small things all at once near the end of the day.

2. Fun. The second thing is that you're loading yourself up with unpleasant tasks. Who wants to face a day of that? Instead, put down tasks that you'll look forward to doing. Create an exciting to-do list for tomorrow. If you really have nothing important to do that's enjoyable, it's possible you're in the wrong job. Look instead for a job that you'll actually enjoy. Yes, every job has unpleasant and difficult tasks, but they lead to something rewarding. They support something you get excited about. If you don't have anything like that in your job, you need to take a closer look at your job—revamp it somehow, or look for another. i

Chapter 21

The Yin And Yang Of Persistence

By Eric Hamm

To be successful in anything you must practice persistence. Without it we would give up the first time we failed. But there's more to it than just having a 'never give up' attitude. In this chapter I want to present you with the different ways of persisting and which ones will help you reach your goals. Is blind persistence a good thing? Should you really 'never give up'? Let's go deeper into the facets of this key act/trait and see how we should be utilizing our abilities to 'push through the pain' so we may reach our goals and obtain our dreams.

But first, let's take a look at the definition of Persisting:

According to dictionary.com Persisting means . . .

1. To be obstinately repetitious, insistent, or tenacious.

2. To hold firmly and steadfastly to a purpose, state, or undertaking despite obstacles, warnings, or setbacks.

I thought these two definitions were very interesting. The first one is representative of persistence in its purest form. Here we see plain and simple tenacity. But if we were to leave it in that pure form without adding some key ingredients it may turn into a 'bull in a china shop' scenario. All power with no control or direction. In comes definition number 2. Here we see the idea of holing to a 'purpose, state, or undertaking despite obstacles, warning, or setbacks.' This one gives a little more direction. It's not just being insistent to be insistent. Here we are talking about being insistent for a purpose.

And it is this that I want to expand on throughout this chapter.

HOW THE PROS BECOME PROS

Previously, I introduced a book I was reading called "Life Is Not A Game Of Perfect." It is an inspiring motivational book written by Dr. Bob Rotella. As a sports psychologist he talks a lot about the different traits he sees in the professional athletes he works/associates with. One such individual is Tom Kite. Tom is a professional golfer who has a quite an impressive career including a win, in 1992, at the U.S. Open.

In the book, Rotella talks about how, as a young boy, Tom used to dream about being a professional golfer and how he pursued that dream quite persistently. But this dream didn't come easily. As Rotella puts it,

"Tom held on to his dream in the face of people who told him he was too small, too nearsighted, and not talented enough."

"He held onto that dream through more than twenty years of disappointments in the majors. He held on to it after he hit a ball into the water to lose his lead in the fourth round of the 1989 U.S. Open. He held on to it through hours and days and years of practicing under the hot Texas sun, rebuilding his swing so that he would not again hit such a shot under pressure.

"And, finally, he won the U.S. Open in 1992."

According to Rotella, it is this persistence that allows us to eventually reach our dreams. He says, "A dream without a commitment is just a fantasy." But persistence alone is not enough.

THE DEFINITION OF INSANITY

You know what they say, insanity is doing the same thing over and over and expecting different results. All too often, people treat their persistence this way. In pursuing their dreams, they try the same thing over and over again and expect the outcome to one day change from a negative to a positive. But the fact of the matter is, if it's not working for you, doing it ten more times won't make a difference. This point was made very effectively in a post I found over at dime-co.com called 'The Truth About Persistence And Success' by Royane Real.

The basic point of the article is the fact that motivational speakers/writers always talk about the importance of persistence in our success, but tend to leave out the need for constant adjustment and re-assessment. As Real puts it, "They forget to tell you that before they were persistent, they had a goal, and they had a plan on how to get there.

"And all along the way, after every step they took, they stepped back to evaluate the results to see if the results they were getting were the results they wanted. And if they weren't getting the results they wanted, then they would change the steps they took.

"These successful people did have persistence, but they were only persistent about holding on to their vision.

"They were never persistent about the method they took to get to their goal.

All along the way, they were prepared to be very flexible and experiment to see what techniques and strategies worked best to get where they wanted to go."

THE YIN AND YANG OF PERSISTENCE

If you read the entire chapter by Rotella and the entire post by Real you will see that they are both talking about the same things but from different perspectives. But I think to pull out these excerpts we are able to see two very important aspects of this valuable trait. In it's pure form you have something that just won't quit. A focus and drive that is not going to let obstacles keep it from reaching it's destination. And yet on the other hand you have a key ingredient that allows for this tenacity to actually *have* it's positive out come.

So to reach your goals and realize your dreams you need persistence to keeps your wheels spinning, but it's flexibility and constant analysis that will take you where you want to go.

"Success is almost totally dependent upon drive and persistence. The extra energy required to make another effort or try another approach is the secret of winning." —Denis Waitley

"Never let your persistence and passion turn into stubbornness and ignorance." —Anthony J. D'Angelo

WHERE DO YOU SEE YOURSELF IN ALL OF THIS?

Do you struggle to keep your wheels spinning? Or do you keep pushing forward, but find yourself too rigid to make the necessary adjustments on the fly? Or have you found the perfect balance of drive and adjustment that have led to great success in life? And if so, what have you found that works for you?

Chapter 22

Enduring the Valley to Get to Success

By Eric Hamm

The path between the starting line and the final destination of your pursuits can be a long and winding road. Hills and valleys are up ahead and the weather is never certain. You stock up for the mission, but uncertainty is at the forefront of your mind as you embark on this very important journey.

When I started my consulting business 5 years ago, I had no idea what to expect. I had heard the statistics, but wasn't too concerned. I figured I was one of the few who would succeed. Looking back, I'm not sure if this was arrogance or ignorance, but somehow I seemed to pull it off.

Coming out of the gate, I was driven by the momentum of my enthusiasm. You could say that I started on a 'hill' and could see all the great potential ahead. I was sprinting with all my mite as I couldn't wait to make up some ground. But it didn't take long for me to find myself in the first valley, unable to see beyond the next bend.

ENDURING THE FIRST VALLEY.

So here I was, experiencing the first real stumbling block of any journey for success. It's in the first valley that many will fail. Not only are you in a low point on the trail, but considering it's your first encounter, you literally have no idea what to expect. It can be petrifying to say the least, and has a tendency to take every last molecule of wind out of your sails.

So what brought me to my first valley?

It was probably a combination of my first bad experience with a client as well as the realization of the work involved in building a successful business. In other words, reality hit me like a ton of bricks. Starting at such a high point and then finding myself tumbling down the mountain, I was experiencing, for the first time, the roller coaster ride to success. Cameron Herold wrote a brilliant guest post on Tim Ferriss's blog that tackled this particular subject. He broke the experience down into 4 steps, with the last one being a juncture that had two possible outcomes. It's called the 'Transition Curve' and it looks something like this:

1. Uninformed Optimism (At a high point . . .)
2. Informed Pessimism (Starting to crash . . .)
3. Crisis of Meaning (Stuck in a valley . . .)
4. And then either 'Crash & Burn' or 'Informed Optimism' (Do I give into failure or take what I've learned and move in a positive direction?) The basic idea is that most of us start this journey with an optimism that is not completely founded in reality. So when reality does finally hit, your drive can take a serious nose dive. Then you find yourself wondering if this really *is* what you want to do or if it is even something that you *can* do. It is at this point that the road splits and you are left to make a potentially life changing decision; "Do I give into failure or do I push through this?" If you choose the latter, you will begin the final step of 'informed optimism' where you will have a positive outlook that is based on facts and not adrenaline. Not only will you continue on your journey, but you will have just gained a very important skill that will be crucial in the many 'miles' ahead.

THE BREAKTHROUGH OF MOVING BEYOND YOUR FIRST VALLEY.

Honestly, I think the fear of being broke was what helped me make the decision to push ahead. But the 'skill' was still learned and the next valley, not as much of a threat.

Many things in life are setup this way. Whether it be the breaking of a bad habit or the pursuit of a dream, making it past the first 'bump in the road' is one of the hardest and most crucial parts of the process. It's the moment the road forks for the first time that you will find out if you want it badly enough.

Your motivators will have their first real test as their ability to drive you is called into question. As I just stated, fear was a big motivator for me in the early stages. This may not be the most 'attractive' drive to admit to, but it served its purpose none the less. So as you start to ascend into this dark, unfamiliar land, know that it is up to you to make it through. Nobody will force you to 'push through the pain.'

6 TIPS TO HELP YOU GET PAST THIS CRUCIAL POINT.

So you're stuck in this valley and are having trouble finding which ways up, let alone knowing how you're going to keep moving forward. I've been there many times and have thus far made it to the next step, so I not only feel your pain, but have some insight that might be helpful.

1. Don't freak out when you realize it's not as easy as you thought it would be. When the initial crash begins to take place, panic is often the first reaction. You start asking yourself, "What am I doing here? I can't do this! This is too hard and just not working out like I thought it would." I can tell you from experience, *this is normal!* Relax and know that this was to be expected. Not because you can't do it, but because your expectations were off to begin with. With a little bit of time and some adjustment to your perspective, you'll be on your way before you know it.

2. Take a weekend and forget all about it. One of the best things you can do to prevent unnecessary panic, is to get away from the situation. Clear your head of the whole matter by taking a weekend and just having some fun. Get some exercise, get some good sleep and relax. Try not to think about what you're going to do, but instead, focus on getting that mind fresh for the week to come.

3. Make sure you're on the right road. After some R&R it's time to ask yourself a very important question, "Is this really the right thing for me to do?" The fact is, often times the reason we fail is because we are attempting something that just isn't for us. You must be careful, though, because this is also an easy time to make excuses and talk yourself out of the *right* path. But be sure this is something your *really* want/need to do. Once you've decided it is, you need to . . .

4. Remind yourself why you started this journey in the first place. Sure, you were pumped with optimistic adrenaline in the beginning, but that doesn't mean the reasons for your pursuit were any less important. Think back to the starting line and re-feed on the ideas for your future. Only this time, do so with your new found appreciation for the challenges that lie ahead.

5. Get advice from a veteran in your field. After you've refreshed your memory, it's time to seek the advice of someone who's been there before. Find that person who's been through many valleys before and keeps rising to the top. Ask for their insight as you . . .

6. Prepare a counter attack. Now that you have the help of a veteran and you are completely convinced that you're on the right path, it's time to layout a game plan to push through this and start your ascension to a successful future. Figure out what things 'pulled the rug out from under you' and learn from the mistakes you had made. Accept the reality of your current obstacles and figure out the best ways around

them. Look at this whole thing as a learning experience, a necessary 'lesson' of life, and make things happen!

Chapter 23

How To Relax And Why It's So Important

By Eric Hamm

Liz and I went to our second of six birthing classes not long ago (in preparation for our little boy). I was reluctant at first, figuring we'd spend the whole time doing that awkward breathing thing, but ever since last weeks initial class, I've been enjoying the learning process. I think all the guys are actually feeling like it's worthwhile and the women are thinking, "You *bet* it's worthwhile! I'm going to need you to step it up and help me get this baby out of me!" (At least that's what Liz says. :-))

We learned something that really stuck with me. This is something that seems to apply to all of life. It was about contractions and the different techniques to getting through them and still sustaining energy until the very end. We talked about how to time them and determine when the woman will be able to relax and when she will be struggling with the pain.v

Then the teacher started pressing on one specific point that she wanted us all to remember and take very seriously. She explained how there will be a point where 'mom' only has between 30 and 60 seconds to relax between the potentially agonizing contractions. She talked about how we naturally want to sulk about how painful the last contraction was while we have our seconds of reprieve. How we naturally think,

"*Man*, that was painful! I don't know if I can do that again! Oh no, here they come again . . ."

She said that instead of wasting this time complaining about the pain that we just experienced and then worrying about what's ahead, that we should utilize this precious rest time to focus on our breathing and work on bringing our bodies to a relaxed state once again. As she further explained, it made perfect sense that if the woman never lets herself experience rest between the contractions, she will be completely exhausted by the time she gets to the crucial pushing stage. Such is life . . .

Life is just like this. There is inevitable pain and suffering wherever we turn. Our pasts are filled with sorrow and our futures bare the brunt of this broken world, leaving us anxious as we wind around the next bend. Yet, there is much beauty and many wonderful things to enjoy in our lives. There are so many opportunities to love those around us, enjoy a sunny day and strive to accomplish great things. It is an impossible paradox to part from.

The fact is, there will also be times when we will need our strength. Times when our families are counting on us to pull through. Our own bodies need us to be strong and fight off the temptations of laziness and self pity. It is absolutely crucial that we maintain our solid footing as we make our way through the ever changing seasons of our lives.

RELAXING IS A SKILL

I am amazed at how many techniques there are to get our minds and bodies to relax. Tapping into the power of our senses and utilizing sight, sound, smell, taste, touch and thought, we are able to recharge ourselves to prepare for the coming storm.

5 SIMPLE TIPS TO HELP YOU RELAX IN THE MOMENT

1. Breathe. Such a simple human habit and yet, if done properly, can quickly bring our blood pressure back down to its optimal state. Deep breaths in through the nose and slow, sustained breathes out through the mouth. Focused, proper breathing techniques are tops on my list of ways to relax.

2. Let go. Often easier said than done, letting go of whatever is bothering us is an essential ability we all need to master. Whether we've been hurt by someone or are just having a bad day, let go of that bad feeling and look ahead. The past is in the past, but the present and the future have yet to be established.

3. Get out! Get outside and get your blood pumping. Whether for a light stroll or a vigorous run, just *get out!* The change of scenery, fresh air and physical activity will almost always leave you more relaxed and better prepared to take on the stresses of life.

4. Read a good book. I hear this advise less and less and I'm guilty of rarely partaking in its beneficial process, but sitting down and reading a book that will take you away to a different world is a very effective way to fend off the frustrations of life.

5. Outward focus. Sometimes we can get caught up in ourselves to the point of poisoning our perspectives. We can become obsessed about what we do or don't have or what did or didn't happen to us. Take a break from this. Focus your attention on someone else and look for opportunities to show that you care. Sometimes the best way to help ourselves is to help another in need. All too often we fail to accomplish this most basic state of mind. Our worries about all things past and future, keep us from relaxing in the present. If we can master this ability and truly take advantage of our time between bouts of life, we can be assured that it will never be too much. But let our minds absorb the poison of 'why' and

'what if' and we will most certainly succumb to the berating blows of our darkest days.

Chapter 24

The Simple Guide To Single-Tasking Success

By Eric Hamm

The multitasking versus single-tasking debate is dead. The fact is, what we consider multitasking is just single-tasking with multiple focus reboots. So I'm not here to debate a dead issue, I'm here to help you become much more efficient and effective in your single-tasking efforts. In this guide to single-tasking success I will be using the good old computer analogy as many can relate to the causes of slow computing and how this is very accurate to our own personal productivity paralysis.

Focus Reboots

A few months ago I published a post called "Minimize Your Focus Reboots". The basic premise of the piece was that just like a computer begins to slow down when it is taking on multiple tasks, so too does our focus begin to bog when we bombard it with multiple mental grabbers at one time. I then took it a step further as I talked about complete focus reboots. When something completely takes us away from the task at hand, we find that our productivity goes out the window. Just like a computer can take forever to reboot, our focus can't just turn off and then back on. We have to go through the reboot process as we reload our thoughts and memories that are essential to the task in question.

SINGLE-TASKING SUCCESS BEGINS WITH BELIEF

If you are not completely convinced that multitasking is a myth and that learning effective single-tasking techniques is the way to productivity progress, then this chapter is not for you. The temptation to multitask is stronger than ever as our

ADHD mentality tells us to take on ten things at once. When I try to tackle a particular task and do so in a singular fashion, it is all I can do not to let my focus wander. Not just out of boredom, but with the unrealistic idea that I can some-how take on more and still maintain my current momentum. Like anything else, if you're not completely convinced of the power that is possible with pure single-tasking, you'll never reach your full productivity potential.

EFFECTIVE SINGLE-TASKING: NOT POSSIBLE WITHOUT PROPER PRIORITIES

One of the reasons we insist on sticking with the myth of multitasking is our fear of forgetting our most important re-sponsibilities. We convince ourselves that if we keep a finger on each of our daily tasks we will never miss that check mark next to its place on our to-do list. The problem with this men-tality is that it requires that we dull our focus. One of the great benefits of effective single-tasking is razor sharp focus that breeds our best results.

To combat this fear and ensure that our most important priorities are properly tended to, we must become expert to-dolisters. I don't care if you use a pen and paper, a website or a whatever form works. The bottom line is that if it's not noted somewhere that task 'A' is to be accomplished before task 'B' and 'C,' we run the risk of a sleepless night as we lay in frustration, pining over our misguided efforts. Take it from me, Mr. ADHD, if I let myself single-task the wrong priority I may find that hours have gone by with no results that needed to occur.

EFFECTIVE SINGLE-TASKING REQUIRES A REWARD

One of the reasons I default to the myth of multitasking is because it allows me to dabble in interests as I also grind out the necessities. The more I purify my single-tasking efforts, the greater the need for a carrot on the end of the stick. Depending on the task, if it's truly being tackled with a singular focus, there is a strong possibility that boredom can swoop in and distract my efforts. My mythical multitasking ways may be diluted with multiple focus reboots, but at least I keep myself entertained.

• The reward of satisfaction. The more we find single-tasking success, the greater our productivity output will become. Each day that ends with our own personal pat on the back will be one more reminder of how good it feels to actually *get things done*. This satisfaction is an excellent carrot to dangle as we push through the pain of a passionless task.

• Mixing it up. As I mentioned earlier, when attempting to do multiple things at one time, I dabbled in both enjoyable and grueling tasks. This was a great tactic for sustained stimulation, but terrible for productivity. So just apply this to proper single-tasking and you've got a great balance that will not only knock out the necessary to-dos, but will keep you coming back for more. (*Tip*: Try to keep the fun tasks from consuming too much time. They're there for a refreshing reward, not a time hungry activity.)

• Clearly define your efforts. Night's, weekends and vacations. What do all these have in common? They represent a clearly defined time to take a break. Our brains need rest and relaxation to fully focus when required. When we blur these lines that separate work from play, we inevitably blur the effectiveness of our focus. Single-tasking, like any other attempt at productivity, will always be performed at it's greatest potential when the proper balance is accomplished.

• Time. Our greatest recourse, time is a precious commodity we cannot afford to waste. And yet we waste so much of it by trying to beat the system. Stick with one thing at a time. You'll get it done, out of the way and off your plate. The reward is easy to see as our time to do what we want will inevitably increase.

DON'T TAKE IT FROM ME, TAKE IT FROM YOUR DELL

Based on the idea that multitasking is a myth and single-tasking is the only way we truly focus, the question turns from 'multitasking or single-tasking?' to 'how to effectively single-task?' But if you're not yet completely convinced of the myth of multitasking effectiveness, just look at the computer you're sitting next to right now (or possibly holding in your hand). Let's say you have a stack of bills that need to be knocked out. You sit down and start hacking away (the computer equivalent to running a virus scan). Though this is purely busywork and requires zero deep thought, your focus still needs room to effectively get it done. Now let's say a friend comes over and starts to chat with you (the computer equivalent to surfing the Internet). What happens? As your friend chats away, your ability to efficiently pay your bills goes *way* down.

Each thought and question that comes out of their mouth takes that much more focus away from the task at hand (as you open your web browser and jump from website to website, your virus scan slows, as does your surfing session.) If you were to tell your friend to come back in a half hour so you could finish your task, you'd be done much quicker and then have a much more meaningful conversation as you are actually able to focus completely on your friend (let the virus scan finish and *then* surf the Net.)

SINGLE-TASKING BENEFIT: ALWAYS MAKE IT TO YOUR DESTINATION

Let's say you're driving down the road, headed toward a specific destination. On the way you decide to take a detour to say hi to a friend. After leaving your friends house you realize how close you are to your favorite ice cream shop. So you stop in and get a sweet treat. A few minutes later, as you start to head back to the main road, you realize that a bathroom break is an absolute must. Now you've got to find the nearest gas station with a bathroom. Unfortunately it's in the opposite direction of your original destination and you just realized the time; *you're late!*

I could go on and on, but you get the point. Often times when we veer off course, we risk failing to reach our destination. The attempt to multitask can easily end up this way. Without the super sharp focus of our target and clarity that only comes from a singular thought process, we're libel to fall prey to this disastrous cycle of distraction.

THE MORE YOU TAKE ON, THE MORE IMPORTANT THIS BECOMES

Recently I launched my affordable web design business. Already having hundreds of local computer consulting clients and a strong connection with this blogging community, I've quickly become busy with business. Almost instantly I realized the downfall of my past multitasking ways. Getting very little done while trying to do five things at once, I bit the bullet and began to dictate my duties with a one-at-a-time directive. All of a sudden my productivity increased substantially as I excitedly checked off my tasks. Instead of waffling back and forth, feeling overwhelmed with a myriad of focus reboots, I could finally breathe. Before I began this new venture, I was able to get by with my attempts to take it on all at once, but now I'm sold on the fact that it is with a single-tasking focus that our greatest productivity prevails.

THE 5 STEPS TO SINGLE-TASKING SUCCESS

To sum it all up, here are 5 steps to make it happen.

1. Pick Your Priorities: As stated above, when picking a task to single out it's always best to start at the top of your priorities. Get done those things that absolutely *need* to get done. Like I said, your sleep depends on it!

2. Limit Your Tasks: Once you've got your priorities straight, it's time to narrow the days tasks to just a few. I like to stick with 2 to 4 must-dos and then mix in 1 or 2 light ones for a break in between. (My ADHD can only handle so much of a single-task.)

3. Remove Distractions: Turn off your phone, email, Twitter, etc . . . Check in a few times if needed, but keep it to a minimum.

4. Track Your Progress: Keep yourself driven by seeing the positive results that follow your single-tasking success. Then, use your charted progress to improve and get more done in the future. It's all about momentum!

5. Clearly Define Your Downtime: At the end of the day/week, we all need to clock-out. Our brains need a clear contrast between work and play. Keep this line well defined and you will be rewarded with your highest level of productivity.

Chapter 25

Stop Reading About It and Do It

By Leo Babauta

We learn more by doing than by reading.

That's a simplified statement, of course, because reading teaches us a lot, but it's in the actual doing of things that we do our real learning. It may be a fairly harmless statement for most of us, but think about this: do you actually put it into practice? How about in your efforts to improve your life?

It's easy to see how this applies in a school situation: In an article in the Chronicle for Higher Education, studies show that the best way to study for an exam is not to read and re-read, but to put the book down, try to recall what you read, then write it down. Much more effective. But how about in your everyday life? This isn't as obvious, but it's just as effective.

When you want to improve your life in some way—by simplifying, by being more frugal, by starting to exercise or eat healthy, by learning more productive habits, by being a more positive or compassionate person—you are learning a new skill.

And when you learn a new skill, all the reading in the world won't teach you the skill. You have to learn by doing.

So reading countless self-help articles and books are great—I've written a few myself—but remember that it's only the first step.

You have to put the personal development posts away, get away from the computer or book, and start doing it. Today. Only in doing it will you actually learn. Reading does help though: first in helping you to understand what to do, and second in keeping you motivated as you actually do the skill. But it's not a substitute for doing.

Now stop reading and go do what you want to learn to do!

Other Great Books by Leo Babauta

If you enjoyed this book and found it useful, you may also be interested in these other terrific, life-changing books by Leo Babauta:

Zen To Done

Zen To Done is a simple system to help you get organized and productive–keeping your life saner and less stressed–with a set of simple habits. Zen To Done takes some of the best aspects of popular productivity systems (GTD, Stephen Covey, and others), then combines and simplifies them, giving you just what you need–and no more. Simply put, ZTD teaches you: (1) The key habits needed to be organized and productive. (2) How to implement these habits. (3) How to organize the habits into a simple system that will keep everything in your life in its place. (4) How to simplify what you need to do. (5) How to implement an even simpler version called Minimal ZTD. If you're tired of doing things the hard way and just want a simple but effective way to accomplish your goals, *Zen To Done* will do the trick. The perfect companion to *The Essential Motivation Handbook.* ISBN 978-1-4341-0318-5

Zen Habits Handbook for Life

A compilation of Leo Babauta's best articles on living from a Zen Habits perspective. Here's the real low-down on how to simplify your life, be happier, be more productive with less stress, and achieve your dreams. The book includes chapters on decluttering, single-tasking, eliminating nonessentials, planning your day, clearing your inbox, getting motivated, cultivating compassion, boosting self-confidence, living consciously, and much more! Think of it as a little handbook for a better life.   ISBN 978-1-4341-0310-9

The Simple Guide to a Minimalist Life

"What is a minimalist life? It's one that is stripped of the unnecessary, to make room for that which gives you joy. It's a removal of clutter in all its forms, leaving you with peace and freedom and lightness. A minimalist values quality, not quantity, in all forms." So writes Leo Babauta, the creator of Zen Habits. A joy to read, this little book will help you clear out clutter, be content with less, and simplify your life–with tips on everything from creating a minimalist workspace to going paperless. In short, it will help you enjoy a simpler, happier life!   ISBN 978-1-4341-0311-6

Focus: A simplicity manifesto in the Age of Distraction

The author writes, "At the heart of this simple book lies the key to many of the struggles we face these days, from being productive and achieving our goals, to getting healthy and fit in the face of fast food and inactivity, to finding simplicity and peace amidst chaos and confusion. That key is itself simple: focus. Our ability to focus will allow us to create in ways that perhaps we haven't in years. It'll allow us to slow down and find peace of mind. It'll allow us to simplify and focus on less-on the essential things, the things that matter most."   ISBN 978-1-4341-0307-9

www.ingramcontent.com/pod-product-compliance
Lightning Source LLC
Chambersburg PA
CBHW060308050426
42448CB00009B/1764